M000166662

THE LOTUS IN THE CITY

Professor David Fontana is a psychologist who holds posts in the University of Wales, Cardiff and the University of Minho, Portugal. He is the author of 16 books which have been translated into 9 languages and he has been lecturing and running workshops for some years. David Fontana has also had extensive experience in broadcasting for national television and radio.

The Lotus in the City

HOW TO COMBINE
SPIRITUAL PRACTICE
WITH EVERYDAY LIFE

DAVID FONTANA

ELEMENT
Shaftesbury, Dorset ● Rockport, Massachusetts
Brisbane, Queensland

© David Fontana 1995

First published in Great Britain in 1995 by
Element Books Limited
Shaftesbury, Dorset SP7 8BP

Published in the USA in 1995 by
Element Books, Inc.
PO Box 830, Rockport, MA 01966

Published in Australia in 1995 by
Element Books Limited
for Jacaranda Wiley Limited
33 Park Road, Milton, Brisbane 4064

Cover Art is the painting *American Buddha* by Rob Schouten © 1988
Cover design by Max Fairbrother
Page design by Roger Lightfoot
Typeset by ABM Typographics Ltd, Hull
Printed and Bound in Great Britain by Hartnolls Limited, Bodmin, Cornwall.

British Library Cataloguing in Publication
data available

Library of Congress Cataloging in Publication Data
Fontana, David.
The lotus in the city: how to experience inner growth
in daily life/David Fontana.
Includes bibliographical references and index.
1. Spiritual life.   I. Title.
BL624.F64 1995
248.4–dc20 95–10501

ISBN 1-85230-573-8

Contents

Introduction

THE POPULARITY of New Age concepts is evidence of the very large numbers of people who wish to live a 'spiritual' life, that is a life which – while it may or may not have anything to do with organized religion – seeks to enhance inner development, to establish intimate and fulfilling relationships with others, to experience harmony with the natural world, and ultimately to discover some meaning and purpose behind human existence. There is no lack of material to help them. From Eastern religions to the Western mystery tradition, from Christianity to psychosynthesis, from yoga to tai chi, from the martial arts to the esoteric traditions, from humanistic and transpersonal psychologies to re-birthing, primal therapy, hypnotherapy, past-life therapy, autogenic training and a vast range of meditation and visualization practices, the individual is bombarded with information, and with teachers and guides who claim to dispense wisdom.

However, what are the essentials that run through the best of these teachings, and how does one reconcile them with the demands and constraints of a busy life in the everyday world – with living with one's family, earning a living and coping with the wide range of values all around us? In past centuries, each aspect of life was potentially informed by a common philosophy, and a shared set of aims and imperatives. But nowadays individuals who set out on the spiritual path are faced with such a bewildering – and, both socially and personally, potentially damaging – conflict of outside obligations and pressures and uncertainties that it can seem well-nigh impossible to decide what spiritual practices are appropriate or even feasible.

The question therefore presents itself: how can we best live a 'spiritual' life within the everyday world? Put symbolically, can we find the lotus flower of spirituality (ultimately of spiritual enlightenment) in the dust of the City? Can we find the space, the motivation, to persevere and at the same time bring up a family, relate to a partner, and hold down a full-time job? How far, for example, are the Christian Ten Commandments or the Buddhist Eightfold Path practical in a modern materialistic society? How can spiritual traditions, which teach self-transcendence, equate with the modern cult of self-seeking and aggrandizement of the ego? What psychological and spiritual practices should we use, and what beliefs are likely to prove helpful? How can we identify the influences that have gone to make us the people we are, and how can we go deeper into our own true nature? And is there an afterlife for which we should be preparing in this life?

Is it necessary to seek a guru and to tramp the roads of the East or retire to a monastery, or can we find a teacher in the City, or an inner teacher who gives us access to our innate wisdom? Are there spiritual benefits to be gained from working in the City as opposed to retiring from the world? How important are meditation, solitude, silence, retreats and pilgrimages, and how does one find time for such things?

The lotus symbolizes the inner world and the progress of inner development, and the City the outer world, with its dust and its distractions. But the lotus and the City are not in reality separate from each other; the lotus symbolizes also the creativity and beauty that the individual can bring to the City, and the City symbolizes the soil that can nurture and feed the lotus. At a deeper level still, the lotus symbolizes the soul, and the City the conscious mind; together they thus stand for spirit and matter working together, and for the fact that ultimately the lotus and the City are part of the same unity, an embodiment of the profound teaching that everything is ultimately part of a creative unity.

As psychological growth and spiritual growth
hand, the search for the lotus is in a real sense a search for
ways of coping with our psychological difficulties and our
personal strengths and weaknesses, as well as about
treading the spiritual path. To grow spiritually is also to
grow psychologically, and develop an understanding of
how each part of ourselves (including the body) can be
brought together in our search for wholeness. So this book
is about psychology as well as about spirituality, and about
the fact that the two are part of the same continuum, rather
than separate (or worse still opposing) aspects of the self.

The reader may find that there is more mention of
Buddhism in the book than of other spiritual traditions.
This is not because I wish to laud Buddhism above other
spiritual paths, but because the guidance it provides for
personal growth, and for investigating our real nature, is
often more specific and more immediately practical than
that given elsewhere. Buddhism, like all the Eastern
religions, is a powerful psychology as well as a path of
spiritual development. In many ways, the psychology it
teaches is far more advanced than that taught in the West
(see, for example, Crook and Fontana 1990), and far better
able to show that psychology and spirituality are aspects of
the same continuous process.

My own credentials for writing this book spring from the
fact that I have from boyhood felt a deep inner longing to
find the lotus of spirituality. I make a few short autobio-
graphical references to this in various places in the book,
and point out some of the early difficulties I encountered as
a result of this longing, but I have tried not to intrude too
much. In my adult life, in addition to long years of study
and practice in Western psychology, I have visited holy
places in those countries such as Greece, Egypt, India and
the Americas that represent the very cradle of spirituality. I
have entered and climbed pyramids, visited holy mountains

and made journeys to great centres of Western pilgrimage such as St Peter's in Rome, Santiago de Compostela in Spain, Walsingham in England and Fatima in Portugal. I have received teachings from the Dalai Lama and other high lamas, and been initiated into various Tibetan spiritual practices. I have been on vipassana, raja yoga and Zen Buddhist retreats, worked with Zen masters, and listened to the wisdom of the Sufis. I have been through the native American sweat lodge ceremony and the Hindu fire ceremony, and have been instructed in the Kaballah. I have followed the Western gnostic tradition on pilgrimages into the Languedoc area of France, visited Greek Orthodox monasteries, Jain temples and the great Gothic cathedrals of Western Europe. I have received teachings in Vedanta, and have studied and practised pranayama, hatha yoga, and tai chi. I know something of the Western mystery and esoteric traditions, have worked with spiritualist mediums, and listened to holy men and women wise in many other traditions.

None of this makes me an expert. But to all these teachings and teachers I owe a deep debt of gratitude. Whatever progress I have made in my search for the lotus is due largely to them. Perhaps the two most important things they have taught me is that the thread of truth leading to the lotus runs through all the great spiritual traditions, and that no matter where one travels and no matter to whom one listens, all teachings are designed to help you sit quietly in your own room. So in my search for the lotus I have never turned my back upon the City. For better or worse, it is where I was born, and where my path lies. It is in the hope that I might help others to sit quietly in their own rooms amid the colour and the confusion and the distractions of the City that this book is written.

INTRODUCTION

A Note on References

There are many references to books throughout the chapters that follow. These have been chosen as likely to be of help to the reader who wishes to study further. There is a danger that references can clutter up the text, so the convention used is to put a date after each author's name, allowing the reader easily to locate the reference concerned in the list provided at the end of the book if he or she wishes to do so.

CHAPTER 1

A Journey Beyond the City

The Journey of Enlightenment

LET US BEGIN with a true story, fairly typical of its type. It comes from the autobiography of the 16th-century Chinese Buddhist master, Han Shan. After spending much of his childhood asking fundamental questions about the meaning of life and death, Han Shan joined a Ch'an (the Chinese form of Zen) Buddhist order at the age of nineteen, and devoted himself to meditating upon the name of Amitābha, the Buddha of Boundless Light, who reigns in a western paradise where the path to enlightenment is easier, and where devotees are said to take their next birth. Han Shan's single-minded dedication to his practice meant that before the year was out he had visions of Amitābha and his two attendant bodhisattvas, thus receiving assurance of his favourable rebirth in the future.

Most beginners would be satisfied with this experience, and continue with their devotions to Amitābha, but Han Shan was after nothing less than full enlightenment in his present lifetime, which involves moving beyond the dualism of subject and object and experiencing that ultimate unity from which all things spring. So he packed his few possessions and set off to receive instruction from a succession of eminent Ch'an masters, one of whom taught him to meditate on the koan (a seemingly insoluble question much used in Zen) 'Who is repeating the Buddha's name?'. Unbroken meditation on the koan for three full months allowed Han Shan to experience that one-pointedness of mind in which the mind abides only within itself, and awareness of the realms of differentiation falls away. Still Han Shan was not satisfied, and at the age of 26 he journeyed to the north to visit Ch'an master Hsio Yen, whose question 'Do you remember the road that led you here?' awoke Han Shan to a realization of the illusory nature of space, and of the fact that the mind truly abides nowhere.

Two years later we find him, still searching, now in the mountains near Beijing, sharing the cave of a revered hermit who lived in meditation and silence. One night, when out walking, Han Shan's forehead seemed to 'burst with a noise like thunder', his body and mind and surroundings vanished, and he became weightless and suffused with indescribable bliss. When he eventually returned and recounted his experiences, the hermit broke his silence to warn him that this was still a manifestation of the material world, the world of form, and that to cling to such manifestations would hinder his quest for ultimate reality.

Once more Han Shan took to the road, and shortly afterwards we catch up with him working on the *Chao Lun*, a sacred Ch'an text, which prompted a further enlightenment in which he realized that 'fundamentally all things neither come nor go'. Even the leaves blown by the wind appeared motionless to him, and flowing waters remained still. All his doubts about birth and death vanished. But one of his teachers warned him that he must still go 'beyond the mind, intellect and consciousness...and above both the saintly and the worldly'. Long months of solitary meditation then led to experiences in which his body and his surroundings were replaced by a great spherical brightness, full and clear as a huge mirror and containing the whole of creation. Han Shan quoted the Sūraṅgama Sutra (see Luk 1971) to describe the experience of this state.

> In utter purity the bright light pervades all,
> With its shining stillness enfolding the great void,
> Worldly things, when closely looked at,
> Are but illusions seen in dreams.

At the age of 40, after much further study and meditation, Han Shan at last achieved full enlightenment, which he expressed in the following lines:

> In clear space and the limpid sea the moon shines
>   on the snow
> Wiping out all traces of the saintly and the worldly.
> When the Eye of Diamond opens, all the flowers in the sky
> Vanish, while the great earth returns to stillness
>   and extinction.

In the above account (see Luk 1971 for more detail), we see Han Shan moving from his early enlightenment experiences, in which form remains (albeit in the person of the buddha Amitābha), through experiences of the absence of thought and of the non-locality of mind, through the emptiness of mind and body, through a realization of the illusory nature of all things, and finally to an experience of the ultimate unity beyond words and descriptions.

The ancient Buddhist masters say that there are 18 major awakenings and numberless minor ones, and as Han Shan's experiences indicate, these awakenings appear to be progressive, each of them stripping away yet another of the illusions which we take to represent ultimate reality. But the question that arises for Westerners on the spiritual path, with careers to follow and families to support, is whether it is possible, without withdrawing from the world as Han Shan did, to experience these 18 awakenings. In any case, perhaps Han Shan and the Buddhist masters are mistaken. Perhaps after all they are complicating things. Perhaps these 18 awakenings are simply facets of the same thing, and if we can achieve the first of them and abide there, the rest will arise of themselves.

This book cannot settle the issue. No book can. Sir Edwin Arnold, in *The Light of Asia* (1971), uses the following words to describe enlightenment.

> The nature of the mind when understood,
> No human words can compass or disclose,
> Enlightenment is naught to be obtained,
> And he that finds it does not say he knows.

Enlightenment is an experience, not a formula. Even great spiritual teachers like Christ and the Buddha either discuss enlightenment (salvation, the Kingdom of Heaven) in terms of analogies and symbols, or refuse to be drawn on its nature at all. They teach instead a path of faith and of practices – faith that there is a quality within us (the Buddha mind, the soul, call it what you will) that transcends the material world of form and appearances; and practices which, if followed, can lead us towards a realization of this quality. Faith and practices. Not blind faith (the Buddha in particular was very clear about this), but a faith that there is a meaning to life if we search hard enough for it. And not half-hearted practices, but a commitment to a way of seeing and relating to the world that pervades each moment, and guides our dealings with others and with ourselves.

An age-old symbol for the search for enlightenment is a journey, a journey which in reality takes us deeper and deeper into ourselves, but which is often represented as (or accompanied by) an outer journey, just as Han Shan tramped the length and breadth of 16th-century China in his search for the path into his own mind. Each time we sit in meditation, each time our thoughts turn to our own spiritual nature, each time we read and study things that help us, each time we try to live our lives with courage and conviction, we are embarking upon that journey. Who knows how long it has taken us – one lifetime, many lifetimes? And who knows how many worlds we have traversed – one world, many worlds? And who knows how long it will be before we reach journey's end, if we ever do? Buddhism talks always of 'beginningless time', and if time has no beginning, then how can it have an end?

The City and the Start of the Journey

Let us assume that, no matter how long we have been travelling, we have idled away much of our time in the midst of the noisy, distracting City. Paradoxically, much of this idleness has taken the form of frantic activity – the activity of building a career, of having fun, of attending to the needs of family and friends – but an activity which has left us with no time to listen to the subtle promptings of the inner self. But now we feel it is time to pick up our belongings (the fewer the better) and set off once more. But set off where? The roads that lead out of the City could be difficult and dangerous. Certainly they will be lonely at times. Why not remain within the comfort and safety of the familiar? All journeys have their hazards. We cannot travel without taking risks. So why travel at all, why not stay and make the best of the pleasures and comforts of the City, and not bother further about vague concepts like the inner self?

The first reason is that the City, for all its attractions, is not a very pleasing place. Buddhism has a term *dhukka*, which is usually translated as 'suffering', but which is perhaps better translated as 'unsatisfactoriness'. Typically much of the City is *dhukka*, unsatisfactory. There are too many tall buildings that shut out the sun and block our view of the far horizon. The roads are busy day and night with traffic, and the air is polluted by dust and fumes. Everywhere is noisy and frantic. We cannot hear the birds sing, and there is little space for greenery and flowering trees. In the winter, the City is too cold, and in the summer it is too hot. The shops are full of overpriced goods that look attractive but fail to keep us happy once we have got them home. The people who pass us in the streets look used up and lost. No, the City is not a particularly pleasant place. It needs transforming with new hope, new life. The boundaries that shut it off from the open country need to be removed. The City is too artificial, too man-made, too divorced from the world as nature made it, the world in which our real roots lie.

The second reason is that we are born with a strange, troublesome quality called imagination. We can *imagine* a different City, a City bounded by open meadows sloping towards a silver river, a City where warm winds carry the scent of wild flowers. We can *imagine* a City looking out onto mountains and wooded valleys and white pathways leading to distant hills, a City which seems to hold the vast sweep of creation in its embrace. Imagination is our constant companion, enchanting and disturbing us. Of all creatures, probably only humans have imagination. Imagination builds dreams and hints at infinite possibilities. In the process it reminds us that the City as we know it destroys dreams, restricts possibilities, and all too often sets each person and each idea against its fellows. So, led by our imagination, there comes a time when, in spite of the loneliness and the uncertainty, we feel the need to set out across the dust and the noise of the City and search for some magic that will transform it into the City of our imagination.

The City is a metaphor for the outside world, but it is also a metaphor for our own conscious minds, minds that are continually tuned into and invaded by the noise and confusion of the City, so that the confusion of the outer world is mirrored by the noise and confusion of our own thoughts, emotions, memories, hopes, regrets and anxieties. The people who live in the City are aspects of ourselves, of our own personalities, and their search for happiness and fulfilment parallels our own search. The

Finding the Time for Daily Practice

People sometimes tell me they have no time to engage in practices for psychological or spiritual growth. The spirit is willing but there are only 24 hours in the day. This objection is reasonable. Modern life is busy, and the more responsibilities we take on, the less time there is for ourselves. All too often we start a practice such as daily meditation, then find it becomes squeezed out, frequently as a result of having to make time to meet the needs of others.

What can or should we do about it? There are no hard and fast rules as to how long our daily practice should last. It is always better to start modestly, and build up from there, rather than to start with an ambitious programme that we cannot possibly maintain. Guidance as to what we should do during our practice (eg meditation, the review of the day, dream analysis) is given throughout the book, but whatever form of practice we use, it must always involve some time spent in silent self-investigation and self-discovery.

The first essential therefore is to have a place where *silence* is possible. Few of us can set aside a room especially for the purpose, so a bedroom is the most likely choice; select a spot that seems right for you, and always sit in that same spot. The second essential is *regularity*. As far as possible, go to your quiet place at the same time each day. Some people prefer the morning, others the evening. Both are suitable. The third essential is to set a *minimum time*, and stick to it. Five minutes a day is enough to start with. Provided the time is well spent, it will lengthen imperceptibly, and soon it will be possible to make a firm commitment to spend between 20 minutes and half an hour (more if you wish) each day.

These three essentials – silence, regularity and a minimum time – are vital to mind training. Without them, you cannot hope to make much progress. But there is a fourth essential, namely to introduce elements of your practice into routine aspects of your daily life. In quiet moments, the mind can be prompted to turn to meditation (Chapter 6) instead of to useless wool-gathering. Self-observation and mindfulness (Chapter 7) can be used wherever possible in place of distracted thinking. Social awareness and social concern can be practised when feasible instead of self-preoccupation.

All these things take time if they are to become habitual. Start in a modest way and build up. Try for example to meditate on the train or bus journey into work, to self-observe for two or three minutes at a set time each afternoon, however busy you are, and to practise social awareness (ie sensitivity towards other people and their feelings) during committee meetings or during encounters with a rather difficult acquaintance or colleague. Be patient but be determined; patience and determination are two of your best friends on your journey.

streets in the City are the pathways we follow in life, many of them leading back time and again to the same place and the same uncertainties. The subways and the dark places of the City are those places within ourselves that we avoid and keep repressed, that frighten and alarm us because they seem outside our understanding and control. The shops full of goods are the possessions we gather in life, each of them fleetingly holding our attention and lifting our spirits before taking its place on the dusty shelves of our personal history.

The Buddha suggested that the problems within our minds arise from three sources: first our grasping and craving, our desire to obtain things and hold on to them for ourselves, to deny the inevitability of change and to keep things always to suit ourselves; secondly, our desire to avoid and push away all the things we find unpleasant; and thirdly our ignorance, that is our failure to understand (or to try to understand) the true nature of things. The Buddha referred to these three sources respectively as *attachment*, *aversion*, and *ignorance*. Through attachment, aversion and ignorance we render ourselves vulnerable to – and in turn create – all that is wrong with both the outer City and the City of the conscious mind.

This brings us back to Han Shan, and the question of how hard we have to search in order to put ourselves to rights. Han Shan, like many of the great masters (I use this term for both men and women throughout the book) in all the great spiritual traditions, devoted his life to the search. For Han Shan there was no office to go to, no mortgage to pay, no family to feed and clothe, no taxes to find, no civic obligations to meet, no qualifications to pursue. Han Shan begged for his food, and as often as not probably went hungry. He wore few clothes, and when the bitter cold became too much for him, he set off on the long road south. His one aim was to find enlightenment, to find God (although a Buddhist would not use that term), to find the meaning behind life and death. And when, at the age of 40, he at last saw into the true nature of things, he spent the rest of his life guiding and teaching others.

Must we emulate Han Shan if we also are to find the truth of our existence – to find it not as a set of beliefs taken over from someone else, but as a deeply lived experience that goes beyond doubt and uncertainty, and reveals who we really are? When asked shortly before his death whether he believed in God, Carl Jung replied that no, he did not believe; then added after a pause: 'I *know*.' How are we to arrive at this knowing, a knowing that enables us to live the truth and not just to believe it to be true?

Carl Jung, like Han Shan, devoted his life to the search,

travelling to far countries and deep within his own mind. I shall have much to say about Carl Jung in the course of this book, because of all modern Western thinkers he touches the deepest levels of the human spirit. Jung was one of Freud's early collaborators, but parted company with him over the latter's extreme emphasis upon the importance of the sex drive in the formation of the personality. Psychiatrist, scholar, author, meditator and mystic, Jung lived a busy professional life right up to his death in his 87th year. He had a wife and children to support, a living to make, clients in therapy to help, a house to maintain (and another one to build as a place for retreat), books and scholarly articles to write, lectures and seminars to give. Yet like Han Shan he transformed the City, and knew well the open countryside around it. Like Han Shan, Carl Jung found the City of the mind to be far greater than anything built by human hands. A few days before his death, he said to a friend:

> Now I know the truth down to a very little bit that is still missing. When I know this too, then I will have died.

This book is about our struggles to follow the paths of Han Shan and Carl Jung, and of the many other men and women who have taken the same journey. It is about doing so, like Carl Jung, in the midst of a busy life and of many obligations. Most of us may not progress far along those paths, but in a sense that is much less important than the fact that we have set out upon them. Some Eastern teachings suggest that at this time in the history of the world, in the so-called *kali-yuga* or iron age, it is much harder to find enlightenment than it was in the golden age, the silver age, and the copper age that are said to have preceded it. Perhaps, unless we are a Han Shan or a Carl Jung, we may not get very far with transforming our City, but if that is the case, then so be it. At least we will have made the attempt, and in that attempt a change in the deep centre of our being will have taken place, an inner transformation not unlike the first stages of that mystical transmutation sought by the medieval alchemists, in which the base metal of the acquired, learnt self is transformed into the pure gold of our own true nature.

CHAPTER 2

─────

Who Builds the City?

Childhood – Before the City

IN THE LAST chapter I mentioned the role played by attachment, aversion and ignorance in creating the problems both in the outer City and in the City of our conscious mind. But almost everyone we meet plays some part in the process: our parents and teachers, our friends, our brothers and sisters, our lovers, and of course the people who tease and bully and victimize us. Not only them, but also the people who write the books and newspapers we read, who make the films we see, who pass the laws that govern us, who preach the sermons we listen to, who hold doors open for us or who slam them shut in our faces. To understand how all this comes about, we must think back to our childhood, a necessary exercise for anyone on the path of psychological and spiritual growth.

For my own part I cannot remember a time during my early years when I was not concerned with unseen things. Underlying the ups and downs of childhood, there was sometimes a strange joy, an inner certainty that life was not bounded by the mortal body. Often the feeling came over me that my mind could know and encompass all things. This could happen at the most mundane of times. Once, sitting at the foot of the stairs as children do, my consciousness expanded outwards until it seemed to become the very centre of everything. Another time, lying on a summer hillside cocooned in the long grass and under a blue and measureless sky, everything became suffused with an extraordinary happiness, as if the hillside and the high summer afternoon were the spontaneous creations of my own mind, and time itself had suspended its breath.

This awareness of the momentary cessation of time was of enormous importance to me, because I was normally acutely conscious of living in a time-haunted world, where each moment slipped through my fingers before I could grasp its magic. Childhood always seemed to me a period of enchantment, so that even during times of sadness I regretted its passing and the fact that existence seemed to dance in an illusive vortex of change and impermanence. There were occasions when I felt an acute longing to hold everything just as it was, with nothing growing older, nothing changing, nothing passing from the present into the past. Why was it, I wondered, that every action, every thought had to take place within time? Why was it that summer vanished into winter, and that we children were such fleeting visitors on life's stage, soon to grow up and leave others to claim our bright, enchanted world?

The strangeness of it all held me captive. Time, space, the world, and perhaps most of all my own life, were deep mysteries so that, like the poet Wordsworth, I was filled with wonder and fear. What was it all, and why was it happening? What was this strange gift called life? What was it to be alive, to breathe, to move, to have thoughts, to dream, to be shaken by intense emotions? What was it, and *why* was it? And why was I me, when I could presumably have been someone else, someone quite different, with different thoughts, and a different life in a different place and time? There were moments when I fancied that everyone else was party to a secret that was hidden from me, that the world was a vast charade played out to deceive me, and that the moment I left a room everyone became once more the insubstantial spirits that were their true nature.

These days of course, working with men and women in

counselling or psychotherapy, I know that many others shared these childhood feelings. I know also that, in spite of the Western myth that childhood is primarily a preparation for the real business of adult life, it in fact contains some of our most valid experiences. Childhood gives us an insight into the nature of the mind before it becomes overburdened with learning and with the ideas and opinions of others. Children experience the world and themselves with a freshness that slips away as we grow older. The truth is that each stage of life should be valued equally. Each stage has its particular strengths and glories. In childhood, these arise from the ability to experience life directly, rather than to become caught up in *ideas* about life. Ideas are excellent in their way, but they can all too easily descend like a veil between us and the actual business of living.

A child lives life with a natural intensity. In childhood, things are as they are, and not as the textbooks describe them. For a child, water is water and not a chemical formula of two parts hydrogen to one part oxygen. For a child, trees, plants and flowers are living experiences, and not botanical specimens. For a child, all things have consciousness, from the pet rabbit in its hutch to the dolls and soft toys in the bedroom and the wind blowing through the garden. Everything pulses with life and awareness, and the child's mind, for all its immaturity, dwells in areas of wisdom that later in life we strive hard to recapture.

Thinking back to our childhood is not only a way of helping us recognize the formative influences that have gone to make us the people we are, but a way of allowing us to glimpse once again some of the things we have lost, and of helping us to see how and why this loss took place. Each of us carries our childhood with us throughout life, and if we wish to continue to grow and flourish we must from time to time listen again to the lessons that childhood has to teach. These issues are returned to in more detail in Chapter 5, but the point to emphasize is that in childhood, the City is not yet fully built, the roads to the countryside are still open, the doors and the gates have not yet been closed and locked.

Walls Built by Religion

Religion should have helped answer many of my childhood questions, but instead, it built many of the walls in my City. I was brought up in a strict Nonconformist sect, and although I defended it stoutly in arguments with my friends, I derived far more disturbance than comfort from it. Just as it seemed that everyone except me might know the secret of existence, so it also seemed that everyone except me was 'saved' (as they called it), and sure of a future in heaven. Everyone else in the chapel we attended seemed secure in their faith, while I seemed always to linger outside, the one person who failed to pass the test or to have the right credentials. This was nothing to do with a feeling of wickedness. I never felt myself to be a particularly bad human being, and I had no evidence (apart from routine skirmishes with adult authority, where generally I felt more sinned against than sinning) that I was badly thought of by others. It was more to do with a spiritual unease, a failure to derive any benefit from chapel, a failure to enjoy the hymns or the long sermons or the piety of my fellow worshippers. Sometimes my unease seemed to sit like a physical weight on my chest, holding me back from participating in what others chose to call the 'fellowship' going on around me. What, I used to wonder, was needed from me?

Why could not I join this 'fellowship', and have done with it? The fact that it did not appeal to me seemed irrelevant. If fault there was, then it must be mine. There was something I lacked, some lesson I had failed to master, like being off school and realizing that everyone but me knew what we were supposed to be doing. Like most children, I could never put any of my deeper thoughts into words. I attended Sunday school and evening service, I wore my best grey suit and combed my hair, I went through the motions with everyone else. I even won prizes for attendance at Sunday school (which should by rights have gone to my mother, who brooked no arguments come Sunday afternoons), and for an absurd few weeks went to evening classes in order to prepare for something called a scripture exam. But still it did not work. I remained excluded from whatever it was to which everyone else was admitted.

Release came suddenly and, it seemed, by my own efforts. I was about nine years old when it occurred to me, quite out of the blue, that the only important thing was whether or not I believed in God. Since I unequivocally did and as far as I knew always had done, there was no problem. It did not matter in the least whether I was like anyone else in the chapel. The things that mattered were inside me, and not outside. As long as I believed in God, I could drop any other worries. I no longer need feel guilty that I was not part of this odd thing called 'fellowship'. It was not my relationship to the chapel that mattered, it was my relationship to God.

And God, on the whole, seemed to me to receive rather scant attention from my fellow worshippers. The talk was always of the Lord Jesus Christ. Christ, with his gentleness, his love and his clear guidance, seemed to me to be a perfect example of how to live one's life, but I wanted to know about God, about the unseen, about what happens in the next life, about ways of knowing and becoming closer to God. It seemed to me that on the rare occasions when God *was* talked about, he was given a very limited sort of existence. People were inclined to speak of what God 'wanted' and what he did not 'want', as if he was a mere human being like the rest of us, with needs and likes and dislikes. They also made him out to be of somewhat uncertain temper, and all too ready to cast the people he himself had created into hideous and eternal damnation.

This did not seem right to me. Christ emphasized that God was love, and referred to him as a heavenly father, and this did not square with an emphasis upon sin and damnation. And if God made us in his own image, where did all the sin and damnation come from? The idea of the devil never seemed very clear to me nor, I suspected, to any of my fellow chapel-goers. I listened to (or more accurately half listened to) sermon after sermon from the pulpit, but none of them seemed to address even remotely the questions I wanted to ask. There was much earnest preaching about the need to live a good life, but this seemed to me so self-evident that I could not see the need to go on talking about it. Often the sermon revolved around obscure texts from the Old Testament, which whatever their content always ended up by proving that if we did not come up to expectation during our few years on earth, our chances of ever seeing God were pretty slim.

Often I sat on the hard chapel chair during a long summer evening, and watched the play of golden light through the open windows, or heard the call of bird song, and wished to be outside, smelling the scents of summer. It seemed to me that this outside world had much more of God in it than the dull space inside the chapel walls.

Walls Built by Science

Soon after the City walls built by religion crumbled away, I found, as we all do, that other walls took their place, built this time by science. Science is a tool of extraordinary usefulness and beauty. It peers into the mysteries of the physical world, finds answers to the most subtle and complex questions, and opens up countless new opportunities for human endeavour. As a psychologist, trained in its ways, I have an enormous respect and admiration for science. The scientific method, which constructs hypotheses, then painstakingly and meticulously tests them against research evidence before reaching informed conclusions, has served us well. As a scientist, I am constantly affronted by the slipshod, random, unscientific way in which many people with power over the lives and the opinions of others arrive at their theories and decisions. In many cases they do so without regard for the facts, and intolerant of the arguments of others.

Yet science has its limits. The things it can do, it does superlatively well (though sometimes its discoveries and its inventions are not put to proper use). But there are many things it cannot do. Science is essentially concerned with the material world; it does not touch the non-material world of thoughts, feelings, values, consciousness and spirituality. These things lie outside its competence, and come within that of the creative arts, of philosophy and of religion in its proper sense. One of the many advantages of being a psychologist is that psychology, perhaps alone of the disciplines, is able to span the divide between science and these other, very different ways of exploring reality. As the study of human behaviour and experience, psychology takes account of all areas of human functioning, sometimes operating as a science, sometimes as an art, and (if it is doing its job properly) always aware of which mode of operation is the more appropriate.

Science builds its constricting City walls when it claims to have the answers to all human questions, when it claims to peer into the very heart of things and to abolish God, the soul, and any life other than our short material existence. In advancing such claims, it ceases to be good science and becomes simply another set of beliefs, as dangerous as those of a fundamentalist religion that claims to know the fate of us all. Many of the greatest scientists have been careful to avoid making any such claims. The Einsteins of this world have a sense of the mystical nature of life which borders upon, and often becomes part of, a spiritual vision. Like Socrates, who was named as the wisest man in all

Athens on the strength of this virtue, they are wise enough to know that they do not know.

Science – or I should say *scientism*, the view of science put forward by scientists who are ignorant of the limits of their own knowledge – built walls for me when it set up an inner conflict between itself and religion. It insisted that science and religion could not both be true, and that whereas the reality of science could be demonstrated, the reality of religion could not. By the time I entered secondary school, all the cleverest boys had, it seemed, rejected religion, and come to regard with scorn anyone who still held such childish ideas. At no time did I ever lose my inner awareness of spiritual truth, but I fought long and hard to try to reconcile this awareness with what was being presented to me as science. Even in my undergraduate days, the fight still went on, and it was only when I knew enough of science to understand both its strengths and its limitations that the fight came to an end. Just as religion had no right to claim that the world is flat or that the sun goes around the earth, so science has no right to claim that there is no God, and that there is no soul within us.

So the walls and towers built by scientism faded first into transparency, and then into non-existence. And with their passing, there was an open space in the City, a space which let in light and helped me to see that the path of science, properly understood, and the path of religion were not doomed to be opposites, the one rational and logical and the other muddled and confused. Both paths were different ways of looking at the many-faceted diamond of life. Without their complementary viewpoints, we risk reducing the diamond to a flat, two-dimensional image, without sparkle and substance.

The Mystery of the Mind

The human mind is as great a mystery as the depths of outer space. In the City, we are often too busy really to

notice our minds. We take them for granted, much as we do
our feet and our hands until they start to give us problems.
Yet the mystery of the mind is every bit as important to the
City dweller as it is to the monk who spends long hours of
meditation each day enquiring into its strangeness. Reflect
for a moment. Where do thoughts come from? One
moment the mind is clear, the next, like a fish leaping out of
water, a thought appears. What constructed this thought?
Where was it constructed? What happened to it before it
entered awareness? And what happens to it when we stop
thinking it? It passes out of the conscious mind, yet the
very fact that it was there influences the thoughts that
follow, and could conceivably change our lives.

Reflect again. How is it that a thought interacts with the
body? Decide to move your arm or your hand or your leg.
What happens? The limb moves, but what is the connection
between the decision and the limb? Now take another area
of the mind, the strange area called memory. Call up a
memory, such as the number or name of your house. Where
was the memory – *what* was the memory – when you were
not thinking about it? And what about memories that lie
even deeper in the mind. You made the journey to and from
school many thousands of times during your childhood.
How many of those journeys can you recall? The average,
even in young undergraduate students who are only
recently out of school, is under 20. Yet if you go on thinking
about these journeys over the next few days, more of them
will come to mind. If you are a good hypnotic subject, and
are regressed into childhood by the hypnotist, you will
remember many more, most of which you will not have
thought about for years, perhaps for decades. Where were
these memories in the meanwhile?

Take yet another area of the mind, that associated with
creativity. Where did the music of a Mozart, Bach or
Beethoven come from? The sublime, uplifting experience of
great music, great painting, great poetry, has its origins in
the human mind. But how? And from where? Similarly

with the great insights and the great ideas of science. Many of these came, not from painstaking observation followed by logical deductions, but in blinding flashes of insight, which then had to be tested in the laboratory (the inductive method) – I've got the answer, now all I need are the facts to fit it, as one great scientist put it.

Sometimes scientism beguiles us with explanations based upon brain functioning, and upon electrochemical activity. We are told that thoughts arise through processes taking place in certain centres of the brain, messages are carried from the brain to the muscles by electrical impulses travelling along nerve pathways, memories are laid down first by electrical stimulation within the brain, and then made more permanent by chemical changes. The problem is that such explanations contain only partial truths. They are like peering under the bonnet of a car and puzzling over the workings of the engine, without any thought for the driver who sits behind the wheel and makes the real decisions. Scientism insists that brain and mind are one and the same thing, in spite of the objections to this notion raised by eminent brain scientists such as Wilder Penfield and Sir John Eccles (see Chapter 16).

Of course, each scientist has a perfect right to his or her own theories on the nature of mind and brain. The problem arises if they insist that science has 'proved' that the two are one and the same. It has done no such thing, and there is a sense in which it can never be able to do such a thing, as the brain can no more fully examine itself than the eye can fully see itself. On a more mundane level, we have no evidence that either electricity or chemicals can contain or transmit thoughts and memories of the kind experienced by the human mind, or that they can experience feelings and emotions, or deliberate upon their own nature, or generate fundamental questions about the meaning and purpose of existence.

If we probe further into the mind, we come upon the mysterious world of dreams, which offers us another life,

parallel and at points intertwined with waking life, yet
following a quite different set of rules, rules drawn not
from our experience of the material world but from some
hidden source deep within ourselves. Even after a lifetime
of living in the realities of the logical, rational outer world,
the dreamer still finds that the dream goes its own way,
offering a separate reality in which one can fly, swim to the
depths of the ocean, die and come back to life, rejuvenate,
cast spells, walk through walls and speak with the dead. In
dreams, animals talk, speeding trains become plodding
horses, trees turn into green men, and the house we have
lived in for years suddenly becomes full of strange echoing
stairways, unfamiliar deserted rooms, and doors through
which we cannot pass.

There are some dreams – all too rare but remembered
with a particular vividness down the years – that transport
us into rarefied realms where we seem to meet the gods,
receive teachings from beings of light, and see a world of
unimaginable beauty. Carl Jung called such dreams 'grand
dreams', and believed they touched the exalted levels of the
spiritual realities deep inside our own selves. But be this as
it may, dreaming takes us into pathways of the mind so far
beyond the usual reach of waking consciousness that we
seem to be transmuted into something greater than
ourselves. The frog becomes a prince, the sleeping princess
awakens, and the magician begins his soaring flight into
eternity. So important are dreams to both our psychological
and our spiritual growth that they are examined in detail in
Chapter 11, together with the other ways in which the City
dweller can look deeper into the mind.

Walls Built by Thinking

Most of us are unaware of the extent to which our habitual
patterns of thinking create the person we are. If we feed
ourselves negative thoughts, full of notions of personal

failure and of bitterness towards others and tow
we see as the unfairness of fate, then we confirm
in our failure and in our bitterness. If on the other hand we
feed ourselves positive thoughts, full of self-belief and of
acceptance and gratitude towards the world, then we
confirm ourselves as effective, confident individuals, able
to make proper use of our potential, and to enhance our
lives and those of others.

By the same token, if we see ourselves as limited,
material beings, bounded by the confines of the physical
body, and the products only of biology and of mechanistic
processes within the brain, then we shut ourselves off from
the possibility of experiences transcending the limits of our
material existence. If we regard imagination, dreaming, the
creative arts and the stirrings of inner awareness as no
more than rather troublesome by-products of the way the
brain happens to work, rather in the way a car engine
produces unwanted noise and heat as a by-product of
power, then we progressively render ourselves deaf to their
subtle whispers.

In other words, we condition ourselves – or are conditioned by those who teach us – to reject a part of
ourselves, the part that sanctifies our humanity, and that
helps bring the conscious and the unconscious aspects of
the mind into proper communion with each other. To give
an analogy, it is as if we live in a beautiful house and deny
ourselves access to the splendid upper rooms through a
refusal to recognize their existence. The house remains,
with the upper rooms flooded with sunlight, and their
open windows looking out onto splendid vistas, but we
spend our lives on the ground floor, even shutting off some
of the finer rooms altogether through misuse and neglect.

Walls Built by Education

And so in various ways the City grows around us. Religion, science, our own refusal to listen properly to ourselves, together with the concerns and stresses of earning our living and trying to make our way in the world, all build walls and high-rise buildings, set up road blocks, build subways that lead us away from the light, cover the green places in concrete, and take down the road signs that point us the way we should go. We complete the process by choking the roads and the streets with the traffic of our thoughts, the constant noise and chatter that occupy each moment of our waking lives, drowning out the silence which enables us to listen to ourselves, demanding and holding our attention, and by turns dominating, stressing and distracting us.

At no time in my education was a word breathed to me or any of my classmates on how to address and control what was happening in our own minds. It was as if the world stopped in that space outside our heads. All that mattered was what was said to us, and what we answered or wrote in our books in reply. At the time, I assumed this was because no one knew anything about what happened inside the head. It was only when, years later, I came to study psychology and, equally importantly, Eastern psycho-spiritual traditions, that I realized that this is not the case. The knowledge, the wisdom is there, it is simply that we fail to consider it important enough to learn for ourselves, or to teach to our children.

More of the City is built for us during our education by the constant emphasis upon thinking of the future, planning ahead, setting long-term goals, deferring present satisfaction in the interests of far-off benefits. Valuable and essential as it is in its way, this constant emphasis upon the future can distract attention away from what we are now. It helps the process, mentioned earlier, of converting childhood simply into a preparation for later life, a kind of warm-up for real living. No wonder that in later life we can never get out of this orientation towards the future, and feel the texture of the present moment. Nature herself never makes this mistake. For her each moment, as it arises, is the eternal present. In her wisdom, she makes no discriminations, and never pretends that any present moment is of any more or of any less importance than any other.

It is all too easy to forget that the present moment is in fact all we have. The past has slipped away, the future has no existence. Life is each present moment, each present breath, each present sensation, each present experience. In the City, our eyes are always on the next turning in the road, on the changing traffic lights, on our watches. The City regulates our lives for us, constantly demanding something from us, criticizing and confusing us, and mocking our attempts to keep up with the crazy pace it insists on setting for us.

Living in the Present

The emphasis in childhood on working and planning for the future also imprints indelibly on our minds the belief that the future will be better than the present, and that being an adult will be better than being a child. The horizon beckons us on, with all sorts of false promises and hopes. We hurry through childhood in anticipation of our bright tomorrows. Small wonder then that one day there comes upon us a sense of disappointment, of being let down. The laughter and the expectations die away. We have arrived and are looking around us, and after all there is very little to see. We experience *dhukka*, that sense of unsatisfactoriness, as if we have suddenly awoken from a dream, and found it to be brighter than reality.

I remember reading in childhood a story of a boy who lived in a house above a valley. Each evening he would sit at his bedroom window and look across the valley to the hills on the other side. Perched high on these hills was another house, tall and imposing, and he would notice how its windows were pure gold, shining and dancing in their brilliance. Entranced by the sight, he told himself that when he grew bigger he would cross the valley and climb the hills on the far side, and visit the house with the golden windows. In his imagination he walked through its hallways and beautiful rooms, marvelling at the golden furniture, at the magnificent carpets, at the pictures on the walls, and at the wide sweep of the staircases. He imagined the people living there, and he heard the voices of kind adults, and the laughter of children.

Eventually he could contain his anticipation no longer. One night, when everyone was asleep, he crept out of his house and set off on his journey across the valley. In the darkness he could no longer see the house with the golden windows, but he knew its location so well he had no need of daylight. Driven on by his great determination he crossed the valley, and began to climb the hills opposite. The way became steep, and often he stumbled and fell in the darkness, but no thought of giving up entered his mind. Soon he would be at the house with the golden windows, and be welcomed into the warmth and comfort within. At last, on the point of exhaustion, he reached the tall gates that led into the grounds of the house, pushed them open, and forgetting his tiredness ran down the tree-lined drive. But when he rounded the last bend and came out on the lawn in front of the house, he stopped short with a cry of bitter disappointment. There were no golden windows after all. Before him was nothing more than an ordinary house, empty and shut up, and with a forlorn, neglected look to it.

He sat down in the porch among the dead leaves, and tried to summon up the strength to make the journey back across the valley. The sun was rising now, and beginning to flood the valley with light. The boy lifted his eyes and looked across to the hills opposite, where his own house stood, and he saw that each of its windows had turned to pure gold. The morning sun shone directly onto them, and each window danced with brilliance. It was the evening sun that turned the windows of the house behind him into gold, and now the morning sun was doing the same to his own house. Much wiser than when he set out, he got slowly to his feet, and started the long journey home.

Walls Built by Emotions

Emotions are tricky things. They provide life with much of its colour. They motivate us to action. They are our joy and our sadness, our anger and our fear, our excitement and our disappointment, our sexuality, our love and our hate. The problem with emotions is that, just like the chatter of our minds, we receive no proper education in how to deal with them. In childhood, we are variously told to control them, to be ashamed of them, or to feel guilty about them. The result is that we repress large parts of them, denying their existence and pushing them down into the unconscious. We are told that we are wicked or naughty to express our real feelings. If we are boys we are told we are unmanly to cry or show our fear. If we are girls we are told it is unfeminine to show aggression or self-assertion. The result is that we become strangers to much of our emotional life. Instead of accepting it, understanding it, and learning to cope with it at a conscious level, for many of us it lurks down in our unconscious, like a dark side of ourselves, ready to break out and overwhelm us if we ever relax our guard.

Freud and his followers linked emotions with the instinctive, animalistic energies that underly the veneer of our conscious, civilized lives. Psychological health can only be gained if we acknowledge these energies, and bring them into consciousness where they can be channelled into acceptable and life-enhancing behaviours. This view stresses again the need for a bridge between the conscious and the unconscious aspects of the mind, so that we become whole human beings, instead of fragmented and divided against ourselves. Carl Jung went further, and saw emotions as linked also to the higher, spiritual part of our natures, which must also be acknowledged and brought into consciousness if we are to realize truly who we are.

Emotions that are denied and misunderstood become the cellars and subways of the City, together with the thoughts that we dare not think and the memories we dare not remember. They are the dark places where we fear to tread, places made even more unpleasant by the garbage of our early traumas, fears and painful memories, which is also dumped down there. Left unattended, these dark places can poison the air of the City, and make it hard to breathe, so that we do not have the lung power, the inner energy, to take down the City walls and start on the processes of reconstruction. Worse still, so much of our attention is taken up in keeping the lid on the dark places, in stopping their contents from spilling up into consciousness, that we even become confused as to what parts of the City require taking down and rebuilding.

Emotions are neither good nor bad in themselves, it is our use of them that makes them so. Even anger and fear, the two most troublesome emotions, have, when properly used, served men and women well. Without the anger that allows us to stand and fight when menaced, and without the fear that prompts us to avoid danger or to run from it, it is certain that the human race would not have survived down the centuries. The problem is not anger and fear, but their misuse by people who have not learnt their proper function, and who become their slaves and their victims instead of their masters. Conversely, love, the finest of all emotions, can be allowed to descend into possessiveness and jealousy when it is used only in the service of one's ⌐, instead of in the service of those we profess to be ⸗ts of our love.

CHAPTER 3

Personality and Spirituality

Personality-Types and the Cities They Build

THE THINKING LIFE and the emotional life discussed in the last chapter should go hand in hand, like a road running beside a river, for these two psychological energies contribute much to our personality. We can see this – plus the other important energies involved – if we examine the description of personality given by Carl Jung. This sees us as a mixture of four different energies (or functional modes as Jung preferred to call them). These four modes consist of two pairs of opposites, *thinking* versus *feeling*, and *sensation* versus *intuition*. If we over-emphasize any one of these modes in ourselves, we neglect its opposite. Thus a man or woman who over-emphasizes the thinking function, and who in consequence is excessively concerned with facts and with knowing, will pay little heed to the feeling side of his or her nature, with its concern for values and sensitivity. By contrast, the person who over-emphasizes the feeling function will pay insufficient attention to the thinking side.

Note that to over-emphasize the one mode does not mean that the other becomes irrelevant. Rather it means that we are out of proper contact with it, and therefore unable to cope with it appropriately. We can notice this for example in the university professor who is a genius at thinking, but quite unable to handle matters related to feeling, or the artist who is steeped in matters of feeling, but unable to master problems which demand objective and systematic thinking.

Similarly, if we over-emphasize the sensation mode, with its concern with the senses and with conscious proof, we under-emphasize the intuitive side of our nature, with its openness to personal insights and hunches. And if we over-emphasize the intuition mode, we become remote from the sensory world, with its beauty and its challenges. The well-balanced individual will be able to operate as appropriate in all four of these functional modes, but most people tend to stress one member of each pair at the expense of the other. Those who stress thinking and sensation at the expense of feeling and intuition tend to be too hard-nosed, rational and objective in their approach to life, while those who over-emphasize feeling and intuition are inclined to be too caught up in themselves and in their subjective responses to experience.

In addition to these four functional modes, Jung also identified two opposing attitudes towards life, that of the *extrovert*, who is more orientated towards and energized by the external world, and that of the *introvert*, who is more orientated towards and energized by the internal world. The terms extrovert and introvert are now widely used in the Western world, and form a very useful way of thinking about personality and the way in which it operates within the world. In addition to each person having two preferred ways of functioning, they thus also have a preferred attitude, and these two areas of personality can be put together to form what Jung called the *personality-type*. Taking extremes once more, we can say that the thinking-sensing extrovert will be most firmly located in the outer world, and the feeling-intuitive introvert most firmly located in the inner.

We can see the unmistakable signs of our personality-type in the architecture of our City. Extroverts build imposing, colourful, often brash and noisy buildings, introverts build restrained, less overbearing, but sometimes

Reconciling the Opposites

Very few people maintain a perfect balance between all four of the thinking-feeling/sensation-intuition functional modes. Those who are able to do so can enter freely the function most suited to the situation in which they find themselves. Their lives are perfectly attuned to the world, to the benefit both of themselves and of everyone else. However, even well-balanced people usually tend to place a little more emphasis upon two of the functions than upon their opposites. Thus we have thinking-sensing, thinking-intuitive, feeling-sensing and feeling-intuitive people. This is acceptable enough, and self-examination usually allows us to identify to which of these four function-types we belong. Similarly, most people tend towards either the extroverted or the introverted end of the attitude dimension.

However, problems arise if we are so rigidly located at one end of any of these three pairs of opposites that we cannot contact and use the other side of ourselves. This is tantamount to being so right- or left-handed that we can do nothing with our weaker hand. Even if we can contact and use each pole of the three sets of pairs, problems arise if we cannot recognize which pole is required in a given situation (eg if we allow our feelings to dominate us in tackling what is essentially a thinking problem, or vice versa). They can also arise if each function is constantly at war with its opposite, as when our head and our heart are in conflict.

Reconciliation between the opposite sides of ourselves does not come about by forcing ourselves to be somebody we are not. The first step is to recognize that we all have the potential for reconciliation. One element of each pair has been repressed, usually as a result of life experiences. Males for example are often conditioned into the thinking mode, females into the feeling; children who are consistently punished for daydreaming are often conditioned into the sensing mode, children who find the outer world a cold and difficult place are often conditioned into the intuitive. The next step is to recognize that, far from being opposed to each other, the four functional modes and the two attitudes should provide mutual support. For example, in an introverted attitude we often learn things about ourselves that are of value when next we operate in an extroverted state, and when in an extroverted attitude we often have experiences that provide food for thought when next we are introverted.

The third step is to observe our own behaviour (Chapter 7) sufficiently closely to know when we have operated in an inappropriate functional mode or attitude, and to recognize why we did so. We can resolve next time to try out the more appropriate mode or attitude, and to recognize why it feels difficult (if it does). What must we do to make it less difficult? Where are the resistances in ourselves, and why are they there? Once we acknowledge that we have these other sides to ourselves, we are well on the way to reconciliation.

more insipid ones. People with a dominant thinking function go in for geometrical, ordered buildings, those with a dominant feeling function go in for ones that are unpredictable, sometimes ornate, often haphazard. Those with a strong sensation function produce buildings that are substantial, four-square and material, those with a strong intuition function build ones that are enigmatic, shadowy, with a hint of secrecy and mystery but with much confusion.

Look around your City and see what buildings you have

created, and how easy it is to lose your way amongst them. Usually they render your attitude and your functions all too clear to see. Perhaps, on the other hand, there is a something of a confusion of buildings, suggesting that you may have tried to change your style one or more times in your life. Or perhaps, if you are very fortunate, each building has a harmonious blend of all the styles, an individuality about it that speaks of a reconciliation and integration within yourself of each of the pairs of opposites.

If your City falls into this last category, you may not only see wide roads and few walls, you may also recognize that the City and the country beyond complement each other. You may find yourself happy with much of the City, and well able to recognize if any parts need attention, or should be changed or redeveloped. But many people find it hard to obtain a clear view of the City. Wherever they stand, they find themselves hemmed in, and their lines of sight obstructed. They long for a place of openness and stillness, from which they can observe everything that is going on, and see more deeply into themselves. Only then will they be able to make the City a living place of colour and joy.

Temperament and Spirituality

If even well-balanced people usually place more emphasis upon certain of the personality functions than their opposites, what implications does this have for our choice of spiritual path, and for our attempts to integrate spirituality with daily life? The choice of path is discussed more fully in Chapter 15, but temperament does have a very marked influence upon the beliefs and practices most suited to us. We might suppose that this means that extroverts and sensationists are more suited to spiritual pathways within the City, because of their liking for social contact and for varied stimuli and activity, while introverts and intuitives, with their preference for a quieter, more inward-looking life, are more suited to the path of withdrawal, even if it leads to the monastery.

However, broad generalizations of this kind are mistaken for all manner of reasons, one of the most important of which is that the close emotional relationships that are often at least as important to introverts and intuitives as they are to extroverts and sensationists are a feature of the City and not of the monastery. The same is true of the careers, the interests, the ways of living and of thinking, and the personal freedoms so important to most of us whatever our temperaments. In any case, as hardly any of us are going to live in monasteries, and as this book is about the City, our concern is with the effect of temperament upon spiritual lives within the City.

The Five Yogas

One of the most useful contexts within which to discuss the relationship between temperament and spirituality in daily life is the Hindu concept of the various yogas (the term *yoga* is from a Sanskrit word meaning 'yoke' or 'union' – the yoke or union between man and God). There are many forms of yoga, but the best known are *hatha yoga*, which seeks to transmute the subtle energies of the body into spiritual energies, *raja yoga*, which uses the non-physical powers of the mind, focused and clarified through meditation, *karma yoga*, which is the yoga brought about by good works and by service to one's fellow beings, *gnana yoga* (sometimes spelt *jnana*), which utilizes the power of thought in order to arouse intuitive wisdom, and *bhakti yoga*, the yoga of devotion.

Whatever our temperament, karma yoga is obviously ⸱ as it involves being of use to friends and and identifying ways in which we can benefit in general. However, the form that our karma

Which Yoga?

As explained in the text, much depends upon temperament. At times, much may also depend upon the
teacher. If we find a good teacher who inspires us, we
may wish to be drawn increasingly into the yoga
taught by him or her, though here again we should not
force ourselves to be someone we are not, or to
commit ourselves too abruptly to the path concerned.
A good teacher will always allow us to work at our
own pace rather than expect us to conform to some
preordained timetable, and a good teacher will be
wise enough and perceptive enough to know what
that pace is.

However, if you are unsure where your own
temperament leads you, your answers to the following
brief questions may help:

- Are you generally more orientated towards outer
  than to inner experience?

- Do you prefer actions to words?

- Are you intrigued by ideas and your own creative
  mind?

- Are you dissatisfied when not allowed to use your
  intellect?

- Do you particularly enjoy working with the body?

- Are you very conscious of the flow and use of
  physical energies?

- Do you feel a special response to the wonderful
  colours, music, symbolism and ritual of the rites
  practised in certain spiritual traditions?

- Are you sometimes overwhelmed by feelings of
  love towards impersonal things such as nature, or

intangible things such as grand ideals or an unseen authority?

- Are you drawn towards the exploration of altered states of consciousness?

- Do you place great premium upon peace and tranquillity?

There are no right and wrong answers to these questions, but if you have answered 'yes' to the first two you may be particularly drawn towards karma yoga, while answering 'yes' to any of the subsequent pairs of questions suggests an inclination towards gnana, hatha, bhakti and raja yoga respectively. In the balanced spiritual life, there is usually an element of all five yogas however, and because we feel drawn most strongly to one of them does not mean that we will not also gain from a study of the others.

yoga takes may vary with temperament. Extroverts and sensationists may prefer to work with groups of people, and to become actively involved in public fund-raising activities and protest movements. Thinking and intuitive types may, in their different ways, prefer to put their energies into the generation of new ideas. Introverts may choose to work behind the scenes, or to engage in activities which, although high profile, do not involve them in the constant round of interacting with new people or with large groups.

Each of these different approaches to karma yoga can be of equal value. There is no need for introverts to feel guilty because they are reluctant to take part in door-to-door collections, or extroverts because they dislike more solitary occupations such as preparing leaflets or arranging mailings. It is often very valuable for our personal growth to engage from time to time in worthwhile occupations that are foreign to our temperament, but on a regular basis we are usually of more benefit to others if we contribute by putting our energies into the things we do best.

Hatha yoga, which involves both individual and group work, can be equally appealing to all personality types. Much depends upon the teacher, and it is worth looking around for a teacher with whose methods you feel comfortable.

Raja yoga, the yoga of mind control, may not appeal to everyone, but it is of value to everyone, no matter what their temperament. The subject is dealt with in detail in Chapter 6, but it is interesting to note that, regardless of temperament, almost everyone with whom I discuss meditation tells me their mind is too out of control to practise it. My reply is that this is the very reason they have need of it. It is precisely because the mind is out of control that the mental training that comes with meditation and similar practices is so important. And however busy the mind, and whatever the temperament, success in these practices is assured provided one uses them seriously and regularly.

In contrast, gnana yoga is not for everyone. As the yoga of *knowledge*, it appeals to those who like to work with ideas, and who are prepared to spend time studying the writings and the philosophies behind the various spiritual traditions. But a word of warning. Although we refer to it as the yoga of knowledge, gnana yoga is more than just knowing a clutch of facts and theories. We should rather refer to it as the yoga of *intuitive wisdom*, because it is concerned not just with ideas that arrive from outside, but with insights that arise from within the mind itself. Outer should speak to inner, and inner should be able to put outer to the test, so that the result is *knowing* and not just knowledge. Gnana yoga therefore demands a blend of thinking and intuition, and the most successful gnana yogis are those who are able to draw equally upon both these sides of the temperament.

In a similar way, bhakti yoga, the yoga of devotion, appeals most to those who can blend feeling and sensation.

Devotion involves both strong feelings of spiritual love, and a sensual response to the rituals and the ceremonies that go with the worship of the divine. Successful bhakti yogis have little need for the study engaged in by the gnana yogi. For them, the reality of the divine is evidenced by the feelings of love the divine inspires within them, and by the powerful emotional appeal of the outer symbols through which the divine is expressed.

The Yogas and the Great Traditions

All five yogas are found in all the great traditions. Even Buddhism, which sees creation as a continuous eternal process rather than the once-and-for-all work of a creator god, contains a strong bhakti element. This is directed at Sakyamuni Buddha (the historical Buddha), at the bodhisattvas and the various deities, and in particular at Amitābha Buddha, the Buddha of Boundless Light, who is said to reign in the Western Paradise where enlightenment can be found more readily than in the City, and where all who call sincerely upon his name will go after death (see Chapter 1). People who are bhakti yogis by temperament generally have a powerful inner need for a personalized divine towards which to direct their devotion. All five yogas are thus relevant in the search for the lotus, and if any one of them leaves us unmoved, it suggests that there is a part of our temperament that is not yet fully acknowledged and developed. But we need make no excuse for placing our primary emphasis upon some of them rather than others. As our spirituality develops, we often find ourselves spontaneously beginning to open to those yogas which hitherto have left us unmoved, but this is not something to be forced. On any journey, we have to start from where we are, not from where we would like to be or from where we feel we ought to be.

If I were asked to select well-known examples of

spiritually advanced men and women who respectively exemplify each of the yogas I would name Mother Teresa, for her work among the poor of Calcutta, as a supreme example of a karma yogi, and Krishnamurti, for his superb ability to seek truth by exposing the falseness of much of our thinking, as a gnana yogi (more is said about Krishnamurti and his methods in Chapter 5). I would name the Indian spiritual master Sai Baba as the peerless exemplar of bhakti yoga (in fact Sai Baba describes bhakti yoga as the most suitable yoga for redeeming our degenerate age), and Iyengar as perhaps the best-known current example of a hatha yogi. As for raja yoga (or raj yoga as it is sometimes spelt), among the very many excellent examples I would nominate a whole movement, the Brahma Kumaris, who take their inspiration from the life and works of the late Brahma Baba, and who have done so much to bring the benefits of raja yoga into the lives of ordinary men and women worldwide.

Each of the above examples could be taken to represent any or in some cases all the five yogas, but each of them is particularly associated with the one with which I have linked their name. Each can serve as an inspiration to us in the particular yoga to which we feel most strongly drawn, and by studying their lives and their teachings we can obtain much of the guidance we need.

CHAPTER 4

Searching for The Lotus: Myths, Legends and Archetypes

DOWN THE CENTURIES and across all cultures, men and women have expressed their longing for spiritual development in the form of a search, a search for a sense of meaning and purpose beyond that furnished by outer experience. There is no evolutionary reason for this search. As far as we know, the human race would have survived very well without it. In fact some evolutionists see it as something of a handicap, in that it may have diverted attention away from the immediacy of securing a living and ensuring physical survival. Some scientists suggest that the search for a reality greater than that discoverable by our physical senses is simply an overhang from an ignorant, superstitious age, when we attempted to explain natural phenomena in terms of superhuman beings and divine powers. Others see it as wishful thinking, an outgrowth of the fear of death and of the annihilation of the self.

However, neither of these views arises from a deep study of spirituality, and of the lives and teachings of spiritually realized men and women. Such a study reveals a picture that has nothing to do with ignorance and superstition, a picture concerned less with explaining the world than with helping us live fruitfully within it, and far less with the survival of the self than with the need to move beyond the self and into a realization that our individuality is only a limited expression of something far richer and more splendid.

Myths and Legends

But let us go back to the search itself. We are in the City, searching for some spiritual meaning in life, while at the same time trying to cope with the business of physical survival among all the demands, distractions and confusions of City life. We are not alone in this. Countless millions of men and women have been trying to do exactly the same thing since the beginning of history. The idea of withdrawing from the City, of living a monastic life, is virtually absent from all except Christian and Buddhist traditions. The other great world religions such as Islam, Judaism and Hinduism have no real place for it (although the faithful do sometimes draw together into more loosely-knit communities). For the overwhelming number of men and women, spirituality and a spiritual way of life are, have been and probably always will be inseparable from the role of householder, family man and woman, and City dweller.

Typically, great teachers have symbolized the attempt to live a spiritual life and to search for meaning while remaining in the world in the form of stories. Such stories, although they may not be actual fact, are true in the sense that they reveal profound insights into human psychology, and symbolically portray the various pitfalls and temptations around us, and how they can be best overcome. Christ used parables, the Buddha used analogies, and there is in all cultures a vast repository of myths and legends that fulfil similar functions. In the West we have Jason travelling to find the Golden Fleece, Perceval seeking the Holy Grail, the maimed Fisher King awaiting the miracle that will heal his stricken kingdom, Hercules embarking upon his twelve labours, Orpheus seeking Eurydice in the underworld,

Merlin in bewitched slumber until the coming of the new age, and countless more. Whether the myth is of searching, of healing or of sleep, the truth behind it is that men and women are incomplete until they discover the hidden treasure of their own true nature.

The great myths and legends of the world, far from being expressions of immaturity, are thus metaphors of psychological and spiritual growth. In most cases they were never intended to represent truths about the outer world, but about inner realities. The tendency in modern times to dismiss them as worthless fantasies, as pre-scientific attempts to explain the world and its creation, dangerously misses the point, and robs us of an essential pathway to deeper self-understanding. Myths arise from what Carl Jung called the *collective unconscious* of mankind (see for example Jung 1966, 1968a and 1968b), that is from the deep level of the mind which is part of our common human inheritance, and which throughout life is the source of all our grander dreams and visions (a point which I touch on again when I discuss dreams in Chapter 11). Myths and legends are representations of our lives, of our relationship with the outer world and with the gods of our inner nature, and of the journey we must take if we are to live in harmony with the former and in understanding with the latter.

Myths and legends are thus guides to the City dweller on how to live a meaningful life. They are the teaching devices of men and women who have faced the very problems that we face, asked the same questions, and experienced the same strivings and the same setbacks and triumphs. These men and women share their wisdom with us in the form of stories because we have always learnt best through stories (even much of modern science is a 'story' in that it is a model of the universe which, though useful and effective, should not pretend to be ultimate truth), and because the deeper experiences of which they speak cannot be put into literal language.

Perennially popular fairy tales often carry something of

The Unconscious Mind

We tend to speak of the unconscious as if it is a single space within the mind, housing that part of our mental life that is not actually in our consciousness at this moment. In fact the unconscious is a vast area, whose beginning consists of the boundary between conscious and unconscious, but whose ultimate borders lie we know not where. The best we can do is to divide it into three levels:

- the *pre-conscious*, which contains everything not in our consciousness at this moment, but which we can recall at will

- the *personal unconscious*, which consists of all our personal life history, much of it inaccessible without such techniques as dream interpretation and psychoanalysis

- the *collective unconscious*, which is that vast ocean of our psychological life which is in our genes at birth, which provides the blueprint of our shared humanity, and which as we go deeper into it may link us with each other through telepathy and other extra-sensory powers, and which may ultimately be the thread that connects us with the divine

It was Freud who recognized the first two of these levels, and Jung who went further and recognized the third. To both Freud and Jung, and to all depth and psychodynamic psychologists, successful communication between the conscious and the various levels of the unconscious is necessary for full psychological and spiritual wellbeing. As the personal unconscious contains all those memories and illicit desires that we do not wish to face or that we repressed during the traumas of childhood, the path into it is difficult. And as some part of the path to the collective unconscious lies through the personal unconscious, the way to establish communication with it may be more difficult still. However, through the techniques of self-exploration, reflection, dream analysis and creative imagination covered in this book, communication with both personal and collective unconscious becomes possible.

The collective unconscious contains much of the energy for our spiritual quest. The creative force that we may variously refer to as divinity, as God, as the great architect, as the great spirit, speaks to us most directly from within it. It is the wellspring of our psychological and spiritual existence, the source through which the boundless and the immortal enters into the bounded and the mortal. As Jung suggests, we cannot know the ineffable energy of the divine in its primal nature, but we can know the form in which it arises into conscious awareness. At the grossest level, this form is of course the human body, but at its most subtle level it is those inner images which we know as the archetypes. These are discussed on page 45.

the symbolic meaning of the great myths. The theme that crops up again and again in such stories is that of a poor peasant boy living in a kingdom suddenly menaced by a dragon or an evil king or by plague or famine or some other calamity. The boy hero hears of a magical object (a sword, a ring, a hidden treasure) which must be found if things are to be put to rights, and he sets off on a perilous journey to find it. On the way there are dark forests to cross, giants and ogres to fight, rivers to ford, and treacherous people to outwit. But he has the help of a wise old man who gives him a talisman to help keep him safe, of a mysterious young woman who uses her magic to guide him, or of talking animals which whisper secrets to him.

Eventually the hero secures the magical object and uses it to right all wrongs and to transform the kingdom into something wiser and more beautiful than ever before. He becomes the new king and marries a princess, or, his task completed, he returns to the forests and mountains of his enchanted journey, and is never seen again. Such a story is a penetrating metaphor for the spiritual quest. The kingdom at the beginning of the story is childhood, the arrival of the dragon or the evil king is the end of innocence and an awakening to the hard realities of the outside world, and the magical journey, with all its perils, is the journey of life – but of a life illuminated by the hero's quest for the magical object of his own true nature. The dark forest is the unconscious, and the various adventures met with by the hero are the pitfalls and temptations of the inner and outer worlds, while the wise old man, the mysterious young woman and the talking animals are metaphors for the mysterious powers of the mind as it goes deeper into itself.

The Archetypes

Jung gave the term *archetypes* (borrowed from early Roman thinkers like Cicero and Pliny, and from St Augustine) to these metaphors such as we have described, and saw them as the personalized form in which the abstract energies of the collective unconscious arise into consciousness. His comprehensive knowledge of comparative religion, and of world mythology, alchemy, astrology, the I Ching and other symbol systems enabled him to identify common archetypal themes and preoccupations, running right across cultures and across the centuries, which provide an esoteric guide to the deeper territories of the mind, and which represent transpersonal and suprapersonal realities inaccessible to the rationalities of conscious thought. James

see Hillman 1990), the contemporary American
_st who founded what is known as archetypal
psychology, describes archetypes as:

> the roots of the soul governing the perspectives we have of
> ourselves and the world. They are the axiomatic, self-evident
> images to which psychic life and our theories about it ever
> return.

Thus the hero is the archetype of our conscious, enlightenment-seeking self (and I have more to say about it below), the wise old man is the archetype of our inner wisdom, the mysterious young woman represents our mystical and intuitive side, and the talking animals our natural, instinctive powers. Other examples of archetypes are the divine child, who symbolizes our purity and innocence (and who is discussed in Chapter 5), the shadow, which stands for the things we fear to be, and the various magicians and gods and goddesses who symbolize our power to transform and change ourselves and our environment, and who at their most exalted are manifestations of the creative force that sustains not only us but the entire universe.

In addition to archetypal objects and characters, there are also archetypal events. These are often associated with the seasons. Spring is the archetype of our own life-giving energies, while winter, the period of darkness and apparent sterility, is the archetype of the incubatory powers of the unconscious, which holds ideas and energies in its womb-like darkness before presenting them to the conscious mind. Autumn is the archetype of change, of transition, of movement from one phase of life to another, while summer is the archetype of full consciousness, when the other seasons have done their work for us, and we are able to enjoy the illumination of mature understanding. The sad thing is that, by removing us from the natural rhythms of nature, our artifical life in the City can also remove us from

contact with these archetypal rhythms within (
and our fellows. We try to cling on to experiences, we forget
that each thing has its season, and that autumn and winter
are as much part of the life cycle as spring and summer. We
fear change, we try to defy the years, we ignore the
meaning of death (a point to which I return in Chapter 16),
we try to insulate ourselves from the natural happenings of
both outer and inner worlds.

The Emergence of the Archetypes into Consciousness

Jung argued that unless the archetypes are allowed to
emerge into consciousness (in stories, in dreams, in
meditation, in religion, in art and poetry) and to be
integrated into our conscious lives, we cannot access all the
inner energies needed for personal growth and for healing
our psychological wounds. This is particularly necessary
during the transitional periods in life, periods which, like
the seasons, are so misunderstood and mishandled in the
artificial world of the City. These include the start of formal
schooling when the child leaves the security of home,
puberty when childhood is transformed into adulthood,
the start of working life, marriage and partnership,
parenthood, retirement and old age. All these mark
profound upheavals in both our outer and our inner lives.
The archetypes are the expression of the inner wisdom and
strengths needed to cope effectively with each of these rites
of passage, the inner potential given us at birth by a mother
nature who knows and provides for these events, just as
she knows and provides for the coming and going of the
seasons.

Archetypal images also appear in the enduring religious
symbols of all cultures: the cross, which is the symbol of the
descent of spirit into flesh, the circle, which stands for
wholeness and the absolute, the square, which represents
the balance of opposites, and the triangle, which is the

symbol of the sacred trinity from which springs the created world (see Fontana 1993). Many other meanings contained in these sacred symbols emerge for us if we take the time to ponder or meditate upon them. Archetypal symbols such as these differ from the signs and logos used as trade marks by commercial organizations in that they spring ready-made from the collective unconscious rather than from the personal unconscious, and thus carry a deep and universal meaning. Emerging as they do from the collective unconscious, they also serve as keys back into it when used correctly.

One of the most potent symbols of all is the flower, that vision of creative beauty that emerges from the secret darkness of the earth. In the West, the form of this symbolic flower is most frequently the rose, especially when placed upon the intersection of the upright and the arms of the cross (the rosicrucian or rosy cross). In the East it is the lotus, whose roots are in the earth, whose stem is in water, whose bud reaches into the air, and whose petals open in the sunlight. Of all symbols of enlightenment, the lotus is one of the most complete, and it is the lotus which in this book represents the magical object which, through inner and outer practice, can emerge into the light of our conscious existence.

The Hero

As I have already mentioned, the hero (for women just as much as for men) is our conscious, enlightenment-seeking self, a self stirred by a divine discontent with materialistic answers to the fundamental questions about life (see Campbell 1988 for a grand survey of his mythological journeyings from the first call to adventure to the final reconciliation with the divine will). Yet – and this is a vital point for the City dweller as opposed to the solitary hermit – the true hero seeks these answers not just for himself but for his fellow men and women also. In his most advanced form, he is thus a symbol of pure altruism, the serving of others with no thought of reward for ourselves.

Altruism of this kind may seem beyond us in our present state. Even when we seek and receive no tangible reward for a good action, we are still recompensed by the warm glow of self-approval that comes from knowing we have benefited our fellows. There is thus an element of selfishness in even the best of our actions. Nevertheless, we need the archetype of the perfect hero as an ideal of altruistic action within the City, and to remind us that, however deeply it may be hidden, we have the same archetypal energy inside us as well. The supreme example of pure altruism was of course Christ's death upon the cross, but a more earthy metaphor is provided by the bodhisattva ideal in Buddhism. The bodhisattva (who must not be confused with the Celestial Bodhisattva, who is a symbol of divine energies) is an ordinary human being who by dint of much striving has reached the state of full enlightenment, and therefore attained the right to enter Nirvana – to pass into that ineffable state beyond the worlds of form and the constant round of birth and death and rebirth. Yet instead of entering Nirvana, the bodhisattva vows to reincarnate time and time again until, it is said, even the very last blade of grass is also free to attain Nirvana.

Having gained the freedom to enter Nirvana, the bodhisattva has nothing more *to* seek or desire for him- or herself. There is literally nothing more to seek or desire. Thus the act of turning aside from Nirvana until all else can enter is an act without vestige of self, an act of pure altruism. Regardless of whether one believes in Nirvana or bodhisattvas, this is a metaphor of the perfect hero. Simply to keep it consciously before one, and to allow it to incubate in the unconscious, is sufficient for it to help open the way for elements of the hero archetype within us to start manifesting in our behaviour.

The great myths of the world are full of bodhisattva-like actions: King Arthur sacrificing himself in the defence of his kingdom; Theseus descending into the grim darkness of the labyrinth to kill the Minotaur and stop the annual sacrifice of young men and women; Prometheus braving the wrath of the gods to give humans the gift of fire; Bellerophon taming the winged horse Pegasus and riding out to fight the destructive lion-headed Chimera; Perseus killing the Gorgon whose very gaze turned mortals to stone. The examples crowd in upon us (Willis 1993 provides an excellent survey).

The hero archetype differs from the god archetype in that he always starts off as a man, with the qualities and frailties of the flesh, and only fully realizes himself when he completes his quest. Reflect upon myths and stories known to you, until you find a version of the hero story that particularly appeals to you. Follow his journeys and attempt to identify the symbolic meaning of each of his adventures and of the people he meets on his way. Use your visual imagination to picture him and even become him. See him as a representative of yourself, and his journeyings and adventures as symbolic representations of your own path.

Becoming the Hero of Your Own Myth

If you wish to work more intensely with your chosen myth, construct a new story around the hero that fits in with what you know of him, but with yourself in the hero role. The story can be very simple, but once you begin work of this kind you will find that your powers of imagination increase dramatically. And imagination is a vital aid to psychological and spiritual progress. Stemming from the unconscious, it provides a path back into the unconscious, thus helping us contact the archetypal energies that dwell there. When constructing your story, there is therefore no need to give too many conscious instructions as to what the story should be about.

Start your story by putting yourself in as relaxed a frame of mind as possible by sitting comfortably, closing your eyes, and checking your body for any signs of tension. Let the awareness sweep the body, working from the feet upwards, and relax any group of muscles that feel tense. Do this two or three times if necessary. Next, bring your awareness to a spot between and just above the eyes. Do not try to visualize a blank screen there. This visualization must be experienced as if from within, rather than as if you are looking at it from outside. Try not to attend to any extraneous thoughts that arise. Keep your concentration steady, but at the same time not too intense. There needs to be something light, almost playful, about work of this kind.

When you feel you are in the right inner space, ask yourself, 'How shall I visualize myself as hero?' Let the unconscious answer the question for you. It may dress you up exactly like your chosen mythical hero, or it may not. No matter. Allow it to be as extravagant or outrageous as it chooses. Do not censor anything. An image may arise of yourself in shining armour, in a uniform of some kind, in the simple clothes of a medieval peasant, as a native American, as a holy man or woman, as a child, even naked as a god or a savage. Your sex, your age, your whole appearance may change. You may find yourself in the guise of a real person you admire, either from history or from modern times. Whatever arises, allow it to be as it is. It is a symbol of the heroic archetype within yourself. Resist the temptation to change it or to interpret its meaning. Accept it as it is. Feel yourself inside it.

Allow this image of yourself as hero to arise as a visualization as often as you wish, although without allowing it to dominate, or to distract you from the business of daily living. See it as that part of you intent upon making progress in the outer and inner worlds, upon exploring and discovering the path of altruism and the deeper mysteries of the self. See it as that part of you determined to live life with wisdom and courage. The image may change as you make progress, often in subtle ways. Allow this to happen. Do not try and hang on to the image too tightly, or to become proud of it. If you do, it becomes detached from the unconscious and serves only as an embellishment of consciousness, feeding the ego and serving to strengthen rather than dismantle the barriers of self-centredness and defensiveness.

Visualizing the City

The City is the symbol of the busy outer world and of your conscious mind as it perceives and interacts with that world. Once you are familiar with yourself as hero and with your personal story-making, imagine yourself entering the City. What do you see? Make no attempt to match your City to the same era as your hero. We are now working in a timeless world. What scenes and images arise? Start by looking at the buildings nearest to you. Are they private houses or shops and offices? Do not make any judgements, or allow your conscious mind to tell you what you *ought* to be seeing. Just see what is there. How do the buildings look? Are they new or old? What is their state of repair? How close together are they? How tall? How inviting or forbidding?

Now start to walk the City. Allow the visualization to surround you, so that you have the idea that even though you are not looking directly at them, the buildings exist behind and on either side of you, as well as in front. Walk where you please, noting whether the streets are wide or narrow, whether they are busy or deserted. Notice whether they are crooked or straight, whether they lead uphill or downhill, and note anything odd or unusual or beautiful about what you are seeing. Notice the dead-end streets,

Contacting the Other Archetypes

You can contact other archetypes in much the same way as you do the hero. Many of them will, in any case, emerge spontaneously while you are working with the latter. We should not use any of them as the starting point of our journey, as it is the hero who represents the archetypal energy undertaking it, but the hero can interact with them, and even change places with them from time to time, as they are all in essence parts of ourselves. For example, we may find that the beautiful young woman, the mistress of mysteries, gives the hero a magic potion, so that his mind merges with hers, and like her he can understand the language of the birds, or cast magic spells to make himself invisible, or conjure enchanted music out of the air.

At such moments, we are fully identified with the intuitive wisdom that the mistress of mysteries represents. The birds are our own instinctive knowledge, the invisibility is our own power to identify less with the demands of the flesh, and the music our own power to bring creative beauty into the world. By the same token, we may become one with the wise old man, and feel ourselves in contact with the accumulated wisdom of the ages, or become one with the divine child and experience all the freshness and innocent wonder with which we first came into the world.

It is important to keep a written record of these inner experiences, as they tend to fade like dreams. Attempt also to draw or paint them, so that the visual imagination is further encouraged (if you feel unable to paint or draw, the book by Betty Edwards listed in the references will soon change your mind for you).

When using the creative imagination to contact the

archetypes, do not waste time wondering whether the experiences involved are 'real' or not. Imagination and reality are not eternal opposites. As will be seen in Chapter 8, imagination can be used directly to affect your body, as in sports performance and in healing. Indirectly, the imagination affects the hearts and minds of men and women by finding creative expression in poetry and the arts, in architecture, and in those scientific theories that spring ready-made into consciousness. (Many scientific theories arrive in this way, after scientific questions have been allowed to incubate in the unconscious.) By taxing yourself with whether inner imaginative experience is 'real' or not, you only raise higher the barriers between the inner and outer world. Leave it that we are created by the experiences of both worlds, so both worlds are our parents, and both worlds deserve our love and our respect.

those blocked off by barriers, those you do not wish to enter, and those that particularly attract you. Walk into the City with all the interest and curiosity that you would experience on visiting a strange town for the first time. Have no preconceptions about what you are likely to see around the next corner. Just walk and look.

Now allow the feeling to arise that you are looking for something, or that there is some task that you have to perform. Whatever the object or the task, it is important you find it. It is something needed by all who live in the City. Perhaps it lies not here but somewhere else; you have no way of knowing. But there may be clues close at hand. What might they be? Where are you likely to find them? Are there people who might be able to help? Who could they be?

In contacting the hero archetype, do not go beyond the

three concepts of yourself as hero, of the City, and of the object or the task for which you are searching. Once the unconscious recognizes that the conscious mind is now open to these three archetypal ideas, it will start to endow them with a creative life of their own, in the same way that the chosen themes of poets are turned into verse by the workings of the imagination. Play mentally with all the images that have arisen – the houses, the streets, the people, the scenes and happenings inside the City. What do they symbolize to you personally? Do not force them to reveal this meaning. Allow it to arise in its own time and in its own way.

Return to the visualization of yourself and the City regularly, without expectations as to how it might develop. You may find that each time the hero – yourself – is back at the same starting point. On other occasions the hero may feel lost, caught up in an endless succession of narrow, seemingly endless streets. At other times there may be a feeling of lassitude or aimlessness, as if the hero needs the energy or the guidance of another person. When this happens, a helper may appear, or may not. Whatever arises in work of this kind, let it arise. Never try and force the imagination. Never decide it is time to move on, or to invent a companion of some kind. Allow the unconscious to do the deciding for you. If nothing happens at all, and the visualizations fail to appear in the mind's eye, no matter. Just stay with the idea of them, as if poised for something to happen. You are waiting until the inhibitions between your conscious and your unconscious begin to fade, and clarity appears. These inhibitions have probably been there since the days when, as children, we were conditioned into repressing the messages of our own creativity. They will not be overcome in a day.

Some people find that once they begin work of this kind, it enters into their dreams, throwing up nightly images that carry the story forward, and provide them with insights they can return to and ponder during waking hours. This is particularly likely to happen if the visualizations are held in consciousness last thing at night, just before sinking into sleep. As we will see in Chapter 11, it is advisable to keep a notebook beside your bed, so that you can record your dreams on waking. Reread your dream notebook frequently, so that something of the dividing line between dream life and waking life begins to disappear. Your dreams, just as much as your waking thoughts and ideas, are the products of your own mind.

Search your dreams for links with the hero archetype and with the idea of the City. Look for any symbolic representations of the object or the task for which you are searching. Look for the emotions that accompany dream images. Do they echo waking feelings you have about the hero, and about the quest upon which the hero is engaged? Remember that the hero is yourself. Everything is connected with your own journey of self-discovery and self-understanding. And be confident that somewhere somehow you have access to all that you need for this journey.

CHAPTER 5

De-Conditioning the Mind: Seeing with Fresh Eyes

The Archetype of the Divine Child

As I SAID IN Chapter 3, the divine child is the archetype of the holy innocence with which we are born. This is not to say that all children are born psychologically equal. Manifestly they are not. Differences in temperament, the raw material from which our personalities are formed, are evident from the early weeks of life onwards. But all children have within them the energy for psychological and spiritual growth, and thus all are at birth in touch with the archetype of the divine child. Christ said of little children 'of such is the Kingdom of Heaven', and Christianity lays particular emphasis upon accepting the Kingdom with the humility and wonder of a little child.

Unfortunately, the experiences to which they are subjected mean that for most children the divine archetype becomes quickly overlaid by the business of living in and relating to the outer world. One of the most destructive features of modern Western society is our failure to honour childhood sufficiently. Childhood is increasingly regarded as no more than a preparation for adult life, to be got through and dispensed with as quickly as possible. And at worst, it is seen as a period of psychological serfdom, in which the individual has no rights to self-determination and self-assertion, and must act as an empty vessel into which the ideas and opinions of others are poured in the guise of objective truth. Little attention is paid to the fact that childhood is not only the most impressionable and formative period of life, it is the time when we are most open to experience both in the outer and inner worlds. The child hears things and sees things to which most adults have become deaf and blind, and to the child there is an immediacy about living which in the adult years becomes buried under concepts and theories. The child lives life at first hand, the adult all too often sees it through a glass very darkly indeed.

Childhood is thus every bit as valid a period of life as adulthood. The fact that it comes chronologically before adulthood does not mean that it carries less value in terms of life experience, or that the child is necessarily inferior in perception and judgement to the adult. I remember as a child being puzzled and disappointed at the adult world. As I listened to adult disputes and adult self-justifications, and felt the heavy weight of adult authority, it seemed to me that there must be a better way of living life. In my years of working with people in teaching and in psychotherapy, I have since found that these memories of childhood puzzlement and disappointment are shared by many of us. Again and again I find that it was in the childhood years that many people feel they were at their most perceptive in terms of their judgements and their emotions.

For those on the path of psychological and spiritual growth, this discussion of childhood is of vital importance for two reasons. The first is that many of us who live in the City are parents (and/or teachers, or work with children in other ways). Thus our spirituality is expressed in many ways through our relationship with our children. Parents sometimes protest that it is impossible to undertake any kind of spiritual practice while they have small children on their hands. This protest is understandable, as our children need our attention and must be our major priority. But far from being incompatible with each other, spiritual practice and the care and love of children could not go more closely together. Spirituality goes hand in hand with a love for, and an understanding of, children. I have never known a good man or woman who was not kind to children. With the deepening sensitivity that comes with spiritual growth, there is always a greater warmth and openness towards children, and an ability to see in them the archetype of the divine child. Spiritually mature people also tend to have a playful, joyful quality about them, which together with their loving nature makes them immediately attractive to children.

The City and the Child

Mention was made in Chapter 2 of the various ways in which the walls in the City are built for us in childhood. In the busy and often artificial life of the City, children are denied the freedom of movement and of experience that come naturally in the rural communities within which we have evolved as a species. The pressures that the City places upon us mean that all too often we can give children neither the time nor the energy they need. The resulting frustrations can make adult-child relationships difficult at times. But with spirituality comes unconditional love, and provided children are assured of this love by parents, most frictions and problems between them can be overcome (some of these points are explored more fully in Fontana 1994a).

The second reason why this discussion of childhood is important is that, whether we currently have responsibility for children or not, we were once children ourselves. And self-understanding, in both the psychological and spiritual sense, depends in large measure upon understanding the way in which our own childhood contributed to the people we now are. This makes us better able to accept ourselves, and better able to identify ways in which we can most fruitfully direct the processes of self-transformation. Thus the following paragraphs apply to us all, whether we are thinking in terms of our relationship with children or in terms of the lasting influence of our own childhood.

Unfortunately, much of the adult world is geared towards stopping children from doing what they want – and often need – to do, and from expressing what they want and need to express. Naturally a child has to learn acceptable social behaviours, but the way many adults treat children reflects the way in which the powerful treat the weak the world over, and in doing so hinder the development of personal freedoms and personal identity. In education, in religion, in politics, in business, in family life, the barriers of negativity are erected at every turn. I am not talking about the necessary constraints that have to be placed upon individual action if social living is to become possible, but the constraints put there because people see themselves threatened by the ideas and abilities of others, or are so sure of their monopoly of the truth that they cannot allow dissent, or feel most significant when in a position to deny opportunities to others.

The Value of Self-Expression

Freud regarded a child's lack of freedom for necessary self-expression as a major cause of neuroses in adult life. Provided we add to this the lack of freedom to value and accept oneself, then I have no quarrel with Freud. In therapy and counselling I have too often seen people who have had some vital force within themselves extinguished by the negative attitudes of others. I have seen too often the hopelessness and lack of ambition suffered by people who have been victimized in this way, and I am always aware that here are individuals who have been given precious human lives, and yet been prevented from living them fully by the selfish and thoughtless actions of others.

Children are not the only victims. Whenever I work with

individuals highly stressed by life in the City, whether they be business executives or houseparents, I see men and women who are being pressured to spend time doing things they do not want to do, or filling roles for which they are unsuited, or collecting responsibilities for which they are not prepared and for which they are ill-equipped. Such men and women speak of being stifled, of being forced to walk down one blind alley after another, and of wasting their lives in trivia when they know full well that there are more important matters beckoning them from quite different directions.

Even as a child I was aware of the disappointment that lay heavily upon the adult world. I heard it in people's voices and I saw it in their faces. Sometimes it seemed to drain the energy from the atmosphere, leaving everything grey and flat. I used to wonder at the lack of enthusiasm for life shown by many adults, at the slowness and heaviness of their movements, at the suspicious watchfulness with which they surveyed the world and each other. I noticed how quick they were to take offence, how ready to attack or to dissolve into tears. Most surprisingly of all, I noticed how little their religion seemed to lift them. They talked of God and of a heaven, yet there was no joy reflected in their words. Even their church services and their hymns – perhaps most of all their hymns – were flat and uninspired, painful dirges that dragged drearily on for verse after verse, suggesting nothing more than a painful duty laid upon the congregation by a God who had also forgotten what it was like to be happy.

I remember how surprised I was when I saw photographs of adults taken back in their childhood. It was only on the strength of this evidence that I realized they had also once been children. From faded photographs they stared out with innocence and hope, caught by the camera in a frozen moment of time before the adult world claimed them and drew them into its lacklustre present. Once upon a time these adults had inhabited the world in which I lived, and had shared the same feelings and dreams. After studying the photographs, I saw the child imprisoned within the adult body, and caught myself wondering whether, if I wished it strongly enough, they could go back into their photographs, and re-emerge as they once were, vivid and real.

Perhaps it was the feeling that adult life could be a prison that made me, even in the most difficult moments of childhood, never want to hurry the years away. It always seemed to me that if only the obstructions that adults built could be removed, the sun would shine full and clear upon the road ahead. I was not sure whether this view was shared by my friends or not, for when we spoke about adults it was in a curiously detached way, as if we were unsure they existed when out of our sight. It is only now, when I talk to adults about their early years, that I realize how much we hide of ourselves in childhood. Most of my friends doubtless had moments of deep unhappiness under their concerns with their games and their bicycles and the life of the outdoors, yet one would rarely have guessed it.

Spirituality as a Way of Life

Children learn far more of practical value from each other than they do from most of the adults in their lives – unless, that is, they are lucky enough to have parents who also know a secret path through the woods, the best place to go for tadpoles in the spring, and for conkers in the autumn, and who know how to make water bombs and produce shrill whistles from a blade of grass. Christ spoke of receiving the Kingdom of Heaven as a little child, and although this carries many levels of meaning, it is as well to remind ourselves that one of these meanings is that spirituality is not grim and serious. Hinduism carries the same message, in its stories of the escapades of the young

Pleasures in the City

Spirituality in the City involves us in entering fully into life, tasting its highs and its lows, rather than in shutting ourselves away in one corner of it – and in one corner of ourselves – and concentrating on being pious. The self-actualized people described in Chapter 9 are all fully and vibrantly alive. In many cases, they have no particular time for organized religion, or for outward show (Christ and the Buddha also spent little time in temples). Their lives, lived nobly, courageously, sensitively and honestly, are their religion.

This shows us clearly that the spiritual life need not be a life of austerity and self-denial. Some may choose this path – it is the path of monasticism and asceticism and achieves results in its own way – but those who choose to follow their spiritual path in the City do so because they wish to find the enlightened mind in the midst of family and the working week, in the midst of the distractions, opportunities and rewards that City life brings. Their path may be the more difficult one, but it is the one they have chosen.

Spirituality therefore does not mean turning one's back upon pleasure. It is not pleasure that is a hindrance, but the circumstances under which one seeks that pleasure (no one on the spiritual path would wish for or could enjoy pleasures that harm or exploit others). We can categorize pleasures as follows (Francis, 1985, provides a fuller discussion).

- *sensual pleasures* that come from an enjoyment of the beauty of the environment, from sport, touch, sexuality, relaxation, and from the physical senses generally

- *mental pleasures* derived from creativity, problem-solving and communication

- *emotional pleasures* that depend upon loving relationships, empathy, excitements and enthusiasms

- *existential pleasures* that arise from achievement, self-value, and feelings of fulfilment

- *spiritual pleasures* that come from inner peace, tranquillity, and an awareness of meaning in life

It is interesting that, although all the five yogas described in Chapter 3 have spirituality as their goal, the temperaments drawn respectively to each of them may similarly be drawn to one of the five pleasures. Thus the hatha yogi may be drawn towards the sensual (for the purposes of control, not indulgence), the gnana yogi to the mental, the bhakti to the emotional, the karma to the existential and the raja to the spiritual. Each of these five pleasures has its place, but hedonism, the pursuit of pleasure as an end in itself, can never lead to happiness or spiritual growth. Even spiritual pleasure is not pursued hedonistically. Pleasure arises, almost incidentally, from one's progress on the path. As one poet put it, on the spiritual path one is 'surprised by joy'.

god Krishna. The Greek gods, with their tendency to visit the world of mortals and share in their various delights, provide other examples.

To live a spiritual life in the City means knowing how to relax and how to play, as well as how to be serious. It means knowing that spirituality is not something to be reserved for our moments of meditation or our hour in the church or the temple once a week. Spirituality is a way of life, a way of seeing the world, of relating to our family and to our work and our friends, and a way of light (it is interesting that in English the word 'light' refers both to ination and to levity). When we speak in Chapter 9 of psychological health and the self-actualized person, we are speaking not of individuals who reserve their spirituality for set occasions or – dare I say it – of people who allow a pious and sanctimonious spirituality to get in the way of living. We are speaking not of people bowed down by the urge to condemn everyone different from themselves, or to preach doom and gloom and to frown upon playfulness. We are talking of people who live natural, open and spontaneous lives, of people who are more concerned with humanity than with dogma, and who set out not to be saints but to be truly and wholly themselves.

In our relationship with our children, this means the ability to see the world through their eyes, and through them to recover again our lost enthusiasm for the natural as opposed to the man-made pleasures of life (and incidentally to allow children to enjoy these natural pleasures themselves; all too frequently these days children are sentenced to a life divorced from nature). Giving time to children is giving time to one of the most important of all spiritual practices. And far from making children more demanding, as some parents fear, this gift of time has the very opposite effect. The demanding child is usually the neglected child, hungry for attention. Children who are confident that their parents enjoy their company and are readily available to them typically grow in consideration and understanding towards the adult world.

The Search Starts in Childhood

All this emphasizes that the search for the lotus of spirituality starts in childhood, and that often children may be closer to finding it than we are in adult life. This raises important questions as to what we need, as spiritually aware parents or caregivers, to teach our children if they are to continue to grow personally and spiritually, and at the same time be prepared for the eventual business of

making their living and facing the challenges and opportunities offered by the world of the City. I mentioned in
Chapter 2 that formal education typically gives the child
little real guidance on how to explore and understand his
or her own mind, or on how to understand and live with
the emotions. The curriculum is heavily orientated outwards rather than inwards.

When the child leaves school, much of what has been
learnt there fades quickly from the mind. This can apply to
mathematical skills, laboriously acquired but never used in
the real world, theories and experiments in science, half-
digested facts in history and geography, fruitless hours in
the craft workshops. So much time, so much effort, so
much anxiety, and so much of it for nothing. Even in higher
education, most of us learn little about personal and
spiritual growth from the formal curriculum. Anything we
do manage to acquire comes largely from friends and from
browsing through the more obscure and disregarded
library shelves. At all levels of formal education, the
purpose of life, the meaning of death, the existence or non-
existence of God, the management of human relationships,
and the care of the earth and its resources are reduced to
mere incidentals, picked up, if at all, more through chance
than through design.

One of the most precious of these incidentals is the
discovery of methods of self-exploration such as the
meditation and mindfulness discussed in Chapter 6 and 7,
and the search for self-identity described in Chapter 8. We
hear much talk of a university education 'training the
mind', but valuable as higher education undoubtedly is in
teaching us how to handle ideas and information and to
learn the languages of the various academic disciplines, it
does little to train the mind to understand itself. Part of our
spiritual practice therefore is not only to undertake this
training on our own behalf, but to help our children to
undertake it. This is done as much through example as
through precept. Such training cannot be forced. But our

own concern for nature and for all that lives, for the value of silence, and for the meaning behind existence, awakens and encourages the child's own feelings for such things. Our readiness to examine our own behaviour, to listen to the child's point of view, to discuss ideas with a concern for truth rather than dogma, to own up to our failings, to answer our child's questions and to encourage further questions, provide additional stimuli for his or her own growth. None of this has anything to do with indoctrination. The concern is to help the child develop openness to the self and to others, and to find for him- or herself the value of the activities of mind that we have been discussing.

Learning to Discard Conditioning

Mention of indoctrination brings me to the subject of its cousin, *conditioning*. There are various forms of conditioning, but essentially the term refers to learning without proper understanding. Conditioning is the creation of powerful associations between certain kinds of actions or thoughts and certain kinds of outcomes. If a particular action or thought habitually brings good results (in the form of praise or material rewards or feelings of self-satisfaction), it becomes an established part of our behaviour, irrespective of whether it has any value or validity in itself. Conversely, actions or thoughts which bring punishment of some kind (whether it be the strictures or disapproval of others or dissatisfaction with the self) tend to disappear from behaviour, again irrespective of whether or not they have value or validity in themselves.

Conditioning in early life, long before we have the knowledge or the self-confidence to explore and reject many of the misguided associations from which it arises, is particularly powerful. Its effects frequently remain with us throughout life unless and until self-exploration is allowed to expose them for what they are. These effects can mean that the child whose interests in spirituality and the deeper meaning of life are met by adult disapproval and ridicule grows up with conditioned and deeply ingrained prejudices against such impossibly whimsical concerns. In the same way, early conditioning often means that boys grow up rejecting as unmanly the gentler, more sensitive side of their nature, while girls grow up conditioned to regard self-assertion and the ability to compete with and surpass their male contemporaries as unfeminine.

Buddhism in particular emphasizes the connection between conditioning and that state of ignorance which it sees as one of the major handicaps to spiritual growth. Because conditioning is learning without proper understanding, it leads to the mechanical repetition of patterns of thought and behaviour which are never examined for truth and usefulness in the light of our life experience. The result is that much of what we do is done without either insight or self-examination. Until we can discard this conditioning, we are likely to spend our lives within the narrow confines into which our minds were manipulated during our most formative years. We are ignorant, the Buddha taught, of our true nature, of the reality that underlies the world of appearances, of the reasons behind our actions, of life after physical death, and of all the other truths of which we are a part but to which we are largely blind. As no one else can do it for us, it is up to us to rid ourselves of this ignorance, and of the conditioning that plays such an important part in its creation. Only then will our eyes open to the lotus flower which has all along been blooming in the dust and mud of the City.

Of all modern spiritual teachers, it is probably Krishnamurti who gives the clearest examples of some of the processes by which ignorance and conditioning can be discarded. There are many books of his teachings, and a good place to start is with *The First and Last Freedom*. For profound insights into the mind of an enlightened being,

Freedom from Conditioning

It takes much effort to follow a spiritual path if we have not first examined and dealt with the things that are holding us back. It is like struggling through a thicket of thorns, instead of pulling up the thorns by the roots and allowing ourselves to walk forward unimpeded. As explained in the text, many of the things that hold us back are due to our conditioning, to that learning without proper understanding that has sunk deep into our minds, and that, without our realizing it, governs much of our action and our thought. Krishnamurti taught that we can never solve the problem of ourselves or of society without first finding clarity within our own minds. This clarity comes about through right thinking (incidentally the first truth on the Noble Eightfold Path of Buddhism). Right thinking leads to right understanding and right self-awareness. 'Without understanding yourself,' says Krishnamurti, 'you have no basis for thought; without self-knowledge, what you think is not true.'

Krishnamurti's approach was meticulously to examine each idea, each concept put forward, not for the purposes of a slick linguistic analysis but in order to probe its living meaning. This can best be demonstrated by looking at how his careful answers to questions turn them back upon themselves. For example, when he was asked how we can act religiously with regard to all things in life (very much the concern of this book) he replied:

We mean by acting religiously...a way of life without division between the worldly and the religious. [Such] division is conflict. A life of conflict is not a religic ... to end conflict needs self-observation and...aw; of the outer as well as the inner. Conflict can c

when there is an understanding of the contradiction in
oneself.

Thus the questioner is left with guidance, but guidance in the form of an identification of the real
meaning of his or her question, and a further question
upon which to ponder ('what is the contradiction
within myself?'). Krishnamurti has stimulated the
activity of mind of the questioner, and has shown the
need for us to find our own answers rather than to take
them ready-made from another, or from a set of
dogmas.

Much of Krishnamurti is very close to Buddhism,
and in particular to Zen Buddhism, where the question
and the answer are ultimately seen as the same. When
a questioner promised to 'think over' his answer to a
question about honesty, Krishnamurti replied, 'Don't
think it over. See it now as it is. From that seeing
something new will happen. But if you think it over you
are back again in the same old trap' – that is in the
same old trap of evasion and dishonesty about
oneself, instead of examining carefully and honestly
what is actually there.

and for the sheer beauty of its prose, one cannot do better
than read *Krishnamurti's Notebook*, while *Krishnamurti's
Journal* also presents some daily records of his inner life.

For the sake both of our children and of ourselves, part of
our search for the lotus of inner development must involve
recognizing when the mind is operating from conditioning
and ignorance, and when it is operating from genuine
learning and understanding. If our true nature and that of
our children is buried under layer upon layer of conditioning and ignorance, then we literally *become* that conditioning and ignorance. Between them they construct for us an

artificial self that, like a crude painting daubed over a masterpiece, bears little relation to who, deep down, we really are.

CHAPTER 6

Concentration, Tranquillity and Insight: The Value of Meditation

WITHOUT PERIODIC ACTS of turning inwards, the mind becomes more and more distracted by external things, and less and less in touch with the resources of its own deeper nature. Meditation is a vital tool for all those in search of the lotus. Meditation is the practice par excellence not only for allowing one to go deeper into the self and to confront the question 'Who am I?' discussed in this and the next chapter, but for training the mind to remain focused and concentrated. It forms the central practice in many Buddhist and Hindu traditions, and has also been an important feature of the Greek and Russian Orthodox churches. Although not much taught and practised in Western Christendom, it was part of the gnostic Christian tradition, condemned and persecuted by the Catholic Church, in which the aspirant sought to have direct knowledge of God.

Why Meditate?

Accessing the hidden territory of the unconscious is therefore part of the purpose of meditation. Meditation allows more and more of the material in the unconscious to become accessible, rather in the way that we hear soft music if we are quiet enough to listen. The unconscious is the source of both our psychological and our spiritual life. It is the wellspring of our creativity, and the storehouse of most of our life-memories. By learning to listen to it, we become more perceptive and more creative. The scope of our memory increases, we grow in self-understanding, and our sense of wholeness and of being connected through these deeper levels of ourselves with the rest of creation increases. As conscious and unconscious mind communicate more with each other, a new equanimity arises, and an increasing ability to observe and understand, rather than be overwhelmed by, unwanted emotional states. The stilling of the conscious mind in meditation, and the progressive ability to listen to the unconscious, also renders us more sensitive to our own intuitive wisdom and the guidance it provides.

Closely linked to these psychological benefits are a number of physical ones. Breathing, heart rate and metabolism slow down, blood pressure often drops, and the brain produces the alpha and even the theta rhythms associated with deep relaxation (see, for example, West 1987). At certain levels, meditation may be even more refreshing than sleep, and serious meditators often need significantly less sleep than usual. Eastern sages who follow very advanced forms of meditation retain consciousness throughout sleep, and the boundaries between sleep and waking virtually disappear.

The prime reason for meditation, however, is to arrive at a resolution to the fundamental existential question, 'Who am I?' This question is, in itself, such a vital part of the spiritual path that it is dealt with in some detail in its own right in Chapters 8 and 9. Meditation is turning the attention away from the concerns of the conscious mind, the chatter of thoughts, the constant bombardment of sensory experiences, and directing it towards the mind itself – which sounds a strange and even impossible thing. Can the mind direct its attention towards itself any more than the eye can direct its vision towards itself? Surely the mind is always *here*, and the object of its attention is always *there*.

Meditation thus brings us up against a paradox. It asks us to do something that looks as if it cannot be done. We live in a world of duality, composed of subject and object. The mind is eternally the subject, and whatever the mind is thinking or attending to is eternally the object. Yet meditation implies that subject and object, observer and observed, can become one. How can this be?

As I emphasize throughout this book, the major spiritual traditions all, at some level in their teaching, stress that there is an essential unity underlying all diversity, and that this unity is the ground of our being. They refer to it variously as Brahman (Hinduism), Nirvana (Buddhism), Ain Soph (Judaism), and the Godhead (Christianity). Furthermore, authoritative voices within these traditions tell us that meditation allows us to experience the truth of this teaching for ourselves. As meditation practice deepens, the mind opens progressively to a reality beyond the diversity of normal, everyday experience, a reality in which the duality of subject and object, the sense of living always in a world composed of opposites, is witnessed as only relative truth. Buddhism has it that:

> When the opposites arise,
> The Buddha-mind is lost.

These lines tell us that if we assume that the separate, distinct, oppositional, material appearance of things represents their ultimate reality, we lose sight of the Buddha-mind. That is, we lose sight of our own enlightened nature, a nature that is not deceived by the illusory world of the senses, and that provides the answer to the question 'Who am I? – an answer which is at the same time the answer to the question 'What is everything else?'

How to Deal with Distractions

Thinking is a powerful and essential tool of the mind, but the problem is that it comes to dominate us, so that for much of the time we experience ourselves as merely a succession of thoughts chasing across the forefront of mental awareness, each one setting off a fresh chain of associations and calling up fresh thoughts, concerns, expectations and so on.

Meditation requires that we refrain from becoming lost in thought. In meditation, thoughts can be observed as they cross the surface of the mind, but we never hold on to them, never judge them or allow them to set off the usual stream of associations. No attempt is made to suppress thoughts, but no attempt is made to attach importance to them or to become involved with them. As the practice of meditation deepens, so one becomes aware that although thoughts are an activity of the mind, and therefore inseparable from it, the mind is more than just its thoughts. Often thoughts even cease to arise for greater or lesser periods of time, so that the mind stays in a state of great clarity, experiencing what is referred to as 'content-less awareness'.

In the same way, meditation adopts a different attitude towards emotions. Just as normally we are caught up in our thinking, so we are caught up in our emotions. Emotions, like thinking, are an important part of being human, but problems arise when, like thinking, they are allowed to dominate the inner life. When working with my clients, I am reminded again and again of the extent to which the mind allows thoughts and emotions to have an apparent life of their own, free to intrude, distract and disturb very much as they please. This raises again and again the question 'Who is in charge of the mind?', for it is certainly not the person him- or herself.

In meditation, emotions, like thoughts, are seen as an activity of mind, and are observed as they arise and subside in just the same way as thoughts, with no judgement or importance attached to them.

It is the same with sounds: the ticking of a clock, the noise of vehicles in the road outside, the ringing of a telephone, voices in the next room, the wind in the trees and the rain on the window. Each of these sounds arises and subsides, passing across the mind like clouds across the sky. No attempt is made to react to them, to suppress them, or to ponder their significance. They are nothing more than events, neither significant nor insignificant in themselves.

In the Tibetan Nyingma tradition, the teacher will suddenly and unpredictably let out a ferocious yell in the meditation hall, or clap two wooden boards together with abrupt force. By watching closely the reactions of the meditators to these events, he or she assesses the quality of their meditation. When first subjected to this, I found it impossible not to be startled, and I fought hard to control this response. Only with time did I learn that a startled response should be watched without judgement like anything else that arose in the mind. With this realization, the reaction lost its sense of importance, and died away. The teacher's yell or the sound of the boards were only sounds, like any other.

Physical sensations are dealt with in the same way. In meditation the body is kept still, as this encourages stillness in the mind. The human body is not comfortable in any one position for long however, and soon demands that an aching leg be moved, or a minor irritation such as an itching nose be attended to. But in meditation physical sensations, like thoughts, emotions and sounds, are simply there. And once no particular importance is attached to them, they begin to lose their claim upon the attention. The meditator discovers the extent to which we empower things through the simple act of noticing their existence. Like unruly children, the more we allow distractions to dominate and disturb, the more they make their presence felt. By contrast, when the mind remains centred in itself

rather than pulled this way and that by each distra‹
begins to experience the tranquil, profound state w....... ...
its own nature.

Imagine a lake or a large sheet of water. When the wind
blows, the surface becomes agitated. When the wind drops,
it becomes still again. The surface agitation is part of the
lake, yet it has no permanent existence in itself. The natural
state of the lake is still and peaceful. And in that stillness
the eye can see deep into the lake, unobstructed by surface
movement.

How to Meditate

When learning to meditate, we must put aside all the rules
about learning gained from our Western education. Meditation is not 'learnt' like other skills, with a body of
knowledge to be acquired, underlying laws to be identified
and committed to memory, tests and examinations to be
passed, and steady progress through a number of clearly
recognizable levels of excellence to be made. In meditation
there are no grades or stars to be gained, no public
commendations to be won, no assurance that our faces will
take on the serene radiance of the Buddha, or that great
truths or beautiful visions will appear.

Meditation starts with concentration. Almost anything
can be chosen as the object of concentration. Some
traditions use the so-called third eye, the position just
above and between the physical eyes. Others use mandalas
or yantras, ie pictures or geometrical designs that carry
deep symbolic meaning. Others use symbols such as the
cross or the crescent, or rupas (images of the gods or saints)
or mantras – words or phrases which are repeated over and
over again, with the mind concentrated upon the sound
rather than the meaning.

Another possibility is the visualization of a god or saint
or teacher in great detail. Or one can use what in Zen

Buddhism is called a koan, a question to which there is no final answer in words, and which is asked as if to someone who sits opposite but who does not speak. However, for many meditators, and certainly for the beginner, the breath is usually the most appropriate thing to use. The meditator places his or her awareness at the opening of the nostrils, where the air is felt cool on the in-breath and warm on the out-breath. The sensation is subtle enough to require concentration, yet not elusive enough to present difficulties. If the mind is particularly active, the breaths can be counted – one to ten on each out-breath, returning to one again after each round of counting (and going back to one should concentration and counting be lost). It is important that the breath is not followed as it flows into the lungs. The concentration must be placed upon the nostrils and must remain there. If the mind is to become still, it must remain in one place, like a sentry never moving from his post (a detailed survey of the various techniques of meditation and how to use them is given in Fontana 1992).

The Effects of Meditation

Concentration is the first step in meditation, and it is followed by two others, namely tranquillity, and insight. I have already likened the mental stillness achieved in meditation to a lake undisturbed by surface agitation. As this stillness develops, so it brings with it a deep tranquillity which meditators variously describe as the relaxation beyond relaxation, an encounter with bliss, and a feeling of coming back home. This tranquillity brings with it a sense of harmony which not only embraces the mind and body, but seems to reach out to embrace the meditation room, loved ones and friends, and even the whole of creation. None of this is recognized in words, because the moment words arise, the tranquillity is lost, and the mind has resumed its habitual activity. It is an experience, and not a

The Koan Exercise

Koans are questions to which there are no satisfactory conceptual answers. 'What is the sound of one hand clapping?' is perhaps the best-known of them, but there are many collections compiled by Zen masters over the centuries, together with the 'answers' and commentaries provided by other masters (eg Sekida 1977). Usually the 'answers' and the commentaries are more enigmatic than the koans themselves, and in fact often serve as fresh koans!

Whatever meditation method we use, we can sometimes work on a koan, and at other times also ponder it. A Zen master will give you the koan most suitable to your level of progress, but 'Who am I?', which is the basis for all koans, is universal.

In instructing me in the use of the koan, a Ch'an master once told me, 'Don't ask yourself for the answer; ask the koan' – ie do not seek a logical answer, keep asking the question. When the answer ('resolution' is a better word) arises, it comes from an area of awareness untouched by rational thought.

This means that the answer is an experience, not a formula. When put into words, it may appear nonsensical to all except the Zen master, who recognizes where it is coming from. Detailed guidance on meditating upon a koan is given by me elsewhere (1991 and 1992) and by others, but here are some simplified instructions.

1 Focus upon the breath until concentration is established.

2 Allow the koan to emerge into the mind, like a silent guest entering the house. Repeat the koan audibly or mentally. If the concentration is good, there can be long pauses between repetitions; if the

concentration tends to wander, the repetitions can be frequent.

3 Keep strongly the 'great spirit of enquiry'. The pressure to *know* is what matters. Do not suppose for a moment that you know what it is you want to know!

4 If logical answers arise, treat them just like any other thoughts; allow them to enter and pass through the mind.

5 As the practice deepens, there is a 'falling away' of body and mind; as one master put it, 'there is something existing there...but one cannot say what it is.' That 'something' may (or may not!) provide you one day with the resolution.

The question 'Who am I?' can also be dealt with conceptually outside meditation, as explained in Chapters 8 and 9. When doing so, the aim is not so much to plumb it to its depths, but to assist one in self-observation, and to identify and strip away the false assumptions one has about one's true identity.

set of thoughts about experience. It is only when the meditation is over that one may choose to think and talk about it.

Tranquillity arises of itself once the mind has reached the appropriate state of stillness. It cannot be willed into being. In fact, attempts to will it are usually a guarantee of failure. The conscious mind is so used to 'doing' things that when tranquillity has once been experienced it enters meditation saying in effect, 'You want to experience tranquillity again, leave it to me and I'll get it for you.' But this is the last thing the conscious mind can do. In meditation, one must sit patiently, expecting nothing and asking for nothing,

concentrating only upon the point of focus.]
tranquillity fails to arise, one must not resolve to try harder
for it next time. Resolve instead to try harder to sharpen the
concentration.

Just as tranquillity arises spontaneously out of the
development of concentration, so insight arises spontaneously out of the development of tranquillity. It can take
many forms, ranging from sudden awareness of aspects of
one's own nature to genuine mystical experiences. Need-
less to say, none of these is grasped or held on to. Whether
long or short in duration, they are simply experienced, and
it is only when the meditation is over that they are thought
about and their effect noted. But too much should not be
said of insight, not only because many aspects of it cannot
be put into words, but because talking about it risks
arousing expectations which then get in the way of genuine
experience.

Advanced meditators may sometimes open themselves
to insights of a particular kind. The attention is turned for
example to any thoughts or emotions that arise. What *are*
thoughts and emotions? Where do they originate within
the mind? Can this point of origin be identified? Or the
point of focus can be shifted to sensations, such as the pain
in the leg or the tickle in the nose. As with thoughts and
emotions, the meditator looks into the nature of these
sensations. They are things we normally take for granted,
judging them only as pleasant or unpleasant. But what are
they in themselves?

In vipassana, the oldest of the Buddhist meditation
practices, the meditator can allow the awareness to explore
in turn each part of the body, registering the slight pressure
of clothes upon the skin, the weight of the body upon the
meditation cushion, the feeling of warmth here and of
coolness there. The result is a sharpening of awareness
which in due course is carried over into daily life. Instead
of passing through the world as if in a confusing dream, the
meditator registers, objectively and without unnecessary

judgement, things missed by other people. The fine
filaments of cause and effect, of similarities and inter-
dependencies, become more and more obvious. Not surprisingly, this experience is referred to in Buddhism as
'seeing into the nature'.

Is a Teacher Necessary?

I am often asked whether we can learn meditation without
a teacher. The simple answer is 'yes'. The meditative mind
is always there, underneath the clutter of our busy lives.
Any moment of stillness, when the attention focuses
without concepts and judgements upon a stimulus of some
kind (a work of art, a beautiful landscape, a candle flame),
allows us to contact this mind. But one of the most useful
roles of the good teacher is to identify whether your
practice is falling into bad habits. Some of these are simply
organizational, and obvious enough – failure to practise
regularly for example, or to set aside a special time in the
day and if possible a special place. Others are more self-
related, such as impatience at a seeming lack of progress, or
a tendency to keep trying new methods instead of giving
one a fair try, or entering meditation with expectations as to
what should happen, and attempting to bring about
desired states through the will.

But a teacher can also help you avoid subtler dangers,
such as becoming lost in contemplation of the visions that
sometimes arise in meditation, instead of treating them as
of no more importance than any other phenomena created
by the mind; or the tendency to slip into a trance-like state,
pleasant enough in itself, but akin to hypnosis (which
involves a relaxation of awareness and an increase in
suggestibility, neither of which have any part to play in
meditation). A teacher will also help clarify points of
technique for you, provide encouragement and also serve
as a good example of the beneficial effects of meditation in

daily life. Remember, though, that a teacher is usually grounded in a particular tradition, and will naturally (and perhaps exclusively) teach the meditation practices of that tradition – which may not be to your liking.

But with or without a teacher, perseverance is important. Do not be tempted to keep changing from one method of meditation to another, first concentrating upon the breath, for example, then using a mantra, then attempting visualization and so on. There is no harm in experimenting, but you must give each chosen method a proper chance. This means at least three months of regular practice. Even experienced meditators may sometimes use more than one method, depending on their needs of the moment. But progress is impossible if you enter meditation with a butterfly mind, always ready to flit to another method or another teacher when the novelty begins to wear off. It is equally important not to change methods during a meditation session (although you may start with the breathing in order to stabilize the mind, before moving to another aspect of your practice). Decide before the session starts what method is to be used, and stay with it. Above all, in all meditation work be patient. Be patient with the method, and be patient with yourself. After many years of mental chatter and indiscipline, once cannot expect to make progress overnight. As the Chinese tai chi masters used to say: 'Start...and continue.'

CHAPTER 7

Looking Where You Are Going: The Value of Mindfulness

Waking up to Life

WE CAN HARDLY expect to find the lotus (or much else of value) if we walk the City with our eyes closed. Various terms are used for the alert state of consciousness that is needed for genuine spiritual growth. For Buddhists it is 'mindfulness', for Gurdjieff it was 'self-remembering', and for gestalt and transpersonal psychologists and New Age thinkers it is more prosaically 'being here now'. Whatever the term, the state involves being properly awake to the moment-by-moment business of living. The command to awake runs like a clarion call through much of the spiritual literature. We find it at the very start of Fitzgerald's inspired (if not always exact) translation of the Sufi classic, The Rubáiyát, of the 11th-century Iranian poet Omar Khayyám.

> Awake! for Morning in the Bowl of Night
> Has flung the Stone that puts the Stars to Flight:
> And Lo! the Hunter of the East has caught
> The Sultán's Turret in a Noose of Light.

These various sources are referring to our need to wake up to our true nature, but they also indicate that in order to do ̖ust first wake up to the business of ordinary living. ̖ddhism tells us that Zen is our ordinary everyday life, and that enlightenment is therefore right here, in front of and within us, rather than existing only in some exalted state after death.

What does waking up to ordinary everyday life actually involve? We can take an example from memory. How often during the course of the day do we find our memory failing us? Not just over big things (though these are annoying enough), but failings over the minutiae of everyday life? Where did we leave the letter we had in our hands a moment ago? What is the name of the person to whom we have just been introduced? Where was it we came across that important reference? What is the title of the book we need? In which shop was it we saw the article we want? What was that important message someone gave us earlier in the morning? What was it we intended to collect from the shops on the way home? What time did we say we would hold that meeting? What is the name of the street we pass each day? What is the date of our friend's birthday? And so on and so on.

Chief among the reasons for these lapses of memory is that we were not paying proper attention in the first place. We were not listening, looking, or thinking properly. Our minds were elsewhere, distracted by other concerns, expectations or plans. We were busy thinking what we wanted to do or say next. The result is that things were not properly registered by the mind in the first place, so they had small chance of being stored in our memory.

Becoming more attentive to our surroundings places us more firmly within the direct experience of living. We become awake to the world, instead of going through much of life half-asleep. If we look at the martial arts (Chapter 14), we find that one of the major benefits they have for spiritual growth is that they teach an intense level of absorbed attention. Martial artists concentrate upon their opponents with every fibre of their being, alert to the tiniest movement on the opponent's part so that their own movement will anticipate it by that fraction of a second needed to gain victory. It is said that through the development of this intense awareness, the martial artist is able to act without the intervention of thought. There is no time for the opponent's movement to be registered by the brain, for the brain to decide on the necessary course of action, and for it then to send a message down to the group of muscles involved. Action must arise in the instant, spontaneously, naturally and correctly.

Spontaneous Action

This ability to act spontaneously should be allowed to pervade many of our actions in life, so that our natural 'goodness of being' can be allowed to emerge into the world, without being continually cribbed and inhibited by the intervention of those patterns of thinking which distance us from the immediacy of the needs of other people. Spontaneity is one of the qualities of the self-actualized person identified by Abraham Maslow (see Chapter 9). There are of course many occasions when we need to think carefully before acting, and there are times when our spontaneous reactions may arise from a misreading of the social or emotional situation in which we find ourselves. We cannot, in the modern, complex world, always trust that our immediate, spontaneous reactions are going to be appropriate. But equally, if we believe that good actions arise not just out of thinking but out of emotions, feelings and, at a deeper level still, out of an innate spiritual awareness of what it means to be human, then we recognize that spontaneous, natural behaviour is imprisoned by the imposition of over-rigid conscious control.

How do we know when the time is right to act spontaneously, or even in some cases whether we *are* acting spontaneously? We can answer the first part of this question by taking the example of spontaneous kindness.

The Practice of Mindfulness

In both my personal development and my stress management workshops I teach the following mindfulness exercise. It amuses some people when they first hear it, but after they have tried it out for a few minutes within the workshop they invariably recognize its effectiveness. I then encourage them to use it as often as possible during their everyday life, for short periods to begin with, then for longer stretches of time. In most cases, their ability to operate mindfully increases so rapidly that they are able to dispense with it quite soon, returning to it only when they find themselves in danger of slipping back into their old, distractable ways.

The exercise is very simple. It consists in keeping up a silent running commentary on everything you happen to be doing, using the word 'now' as often as possible. '*Now* I am picking up that important letter I received this morning, and reading it again. *Now* I am putting it down on my desk, underneath the paperweight, and reminding myself where to find it when I need it later in the day. *Now* I am walking into the kitchen to make coffee. *Now* I am getting out the coffee and the coffee cups, and putting the kettle on. *Now* I can hear the telephone ringing. *Now* I am reminding myself to come back and finish making the coffee as soon as I have answered it.' And so on. This simple exercise does a number of things:

- It keeps the mind focused upon each action.

- It prevents the mind from becoming lost in thought.

- It vastly improves the memory, as the mind is continually aware of what is being done.

- It helps add interest to even the most mundane tasks; a concentrated mind is one of the best defences against boredom.

- It allows the mind to recognize the intrinsic fascination of even the simplest objects, and the beauty and grace that can be identified in even the simplest of movements.

There are other benefits, less easily put into words. As the concentration develops, you may have moments of almost mystical insight into creation and into your relationship with it. You may find the stillness and concentration of the mind produces a tranquillity similar to that in sitting meditation. You may be caught up in a profound sense of the mystery of everything being just as it is (the 'suchness' of things, as the Eastern sages put it). You may have moments of overwhelming gratitude at being alive. Do not attempt the exercise with these expectations in mind. Allow them to come if they will. But whether they do or not, the benefits in terms of greater efficiency in daily life, and of better use of physical and mental energy, are incalculable.

We are most of us fortunate enough to have met individuals whose behaviour is characterized by a generosity of spirit that overflows towards all with whom they come into contact. Such people seem to be naturally good. Their behaviour appears to arise without effort, without thinking, without a constant weighing of the pros and cons before help is offered.

Spontaneous kindness is not part of a 'good boy' or 'good girl' syndrome, in which help is given in order that the donor can feel virtuous about him- or herself. There is an absence of any striving for the 'feel-good' factor, a relic of those experiences in childhood when we were patted on the head and told how good we had been. There is no feeling even that merit is being gained for the next lifetime, or riches stored up in heaven. The behaviour is a hint of the bodhisattva spirit, which was detailed in Chapter 4.

Of course, if we plunge abruptly into an attempt to be spontaneously kind at all times, the result is likely to be an absurd number of impractical commitments that we cannot possibly fulfil. In addition, our actions will have something artificial and contrived about them. We will be doing them in order to be spontaneously kind, rather than because we *are* spontaneously kind. If the behaviour is to be sustainable and genuine, it is therefore generally necessary to proceed step by step. A start can be made by identifying appropriate areas of life (no matter how small) where spontaneous acts of kindness are called for, and then concentrating upon these.

They might include assisting colleagues with known difficulties at work, or helping friends or family in a particular context. For the motorist, they could include extra acts of courtesy towards fellow road-users, and for those dealing with the public additional attempts at being of service. We are so accustomed to linking thought with action that we cannot be expected immediately to eliminate the habit on these or similar occasions. It is quite enough therefore just to avoid the preliminary internal dialogue which all too often ends in excuses as to why we should not act, and to avoid dwelling upon matters afterwards. An occasion for giving help arises, the help is given, the occasion passes, and there is no more to it than that.

Learning to Observe Ourselves

If the whole thing proves too difficult for us, then this is a cue for self-observation, that is, for watching our own mind and identifying the nature and origin of this difficulty. Self-

observation is in any case an essential aspect of mindfulness at all times. We should not only observe the outer
world closely, we should also observe ourselves. The
American psychologist Charles Tart of the University of
California (eg 1988) has stressed the extent to which so
much of our behaviour has become mechanical, as a result
of a number of factors including early conditioning, the
many 'rules' that govern the roles we play in life, and the
various psychological defence mechanisms acquired in
childhood. The sheer efficiency with which we are able to
function without really attending to what we are doing
makes us even more likely to run on what might be called
our internal automatic pilot. The result is that much of our
behaviour becomes a succession of robot-like actions,
unconnected with any but the most primitive levels of
awareness.

It is the internal automatic pilot that allows us to eat our
breakfast or our evening meal while watching television, to
go jogging (or worse still cycling) with the headphones of a
personal stereo clamped to our ears, to read a page of a
book without taking in a word of it, to hold a conversation
without recalling anything that was said, and to walk or
drive home through the same streets night after night
without registering a single road name.

Of course, in the busy life of the City, we cannot make
every action a fully conscious one, in the way that the
Buddhist monk is expected to do. If we are attending to the
details on the road ahead as we drive our car, we should
not also be taking in the details through the side windows.
If we are concentrating on the act of walking, we cannot
also (at least initially) be focusing upon our breathing or the
feel of the wind on our faces. Similarly, when we are
concentrating fully on the act of thinking, we cannot also be
taking in everything that is happening around us. There is
often a sense in which attention has to be selective.
However, in order to be properly awake, the attention
should always be focussed fully upon the central thing that

is occupying us at the time. When driving we should drive, when walking walk, when eating eat, and when thinking think. And as far as possible, we should avoid dividing our attention by trying to do more than one thing at a time. Being properly awake not only makes life far less stressful, it means that we pay direct attention to the reality of the moment-by-moment experience of being alive.

Direct Contemplation

There is an important meditation technique which can be used to help us, known as *direct contemplation*. In its most usual form, it involves using an object as a focus for meditation (any object, though beginners are usually encouraged to start with a natural rather than a man-made one), and concentrating upon it without becoming lost in intervening thoughts. In other words, we allow the object itself, rather than thoughts about the object, to occupy the mind. As we become more proficient in this meditation, so we truly 'see' the object for the first time. People describe this experience of 'seeing' in different ways (see, for example, Deikman 1973). Some suggest that the object takes on a luminosity, a vividness or a beauty never seen before. Others report a decrease in feelings of self–object separation, as if they and the object are part of a single experience. Others speak of an awareness of the life force within the object. One of the greatest of Western mystics, the Hungarian-born Austrian Rudolf Steiner, placed particular emphasis on this form of meditation, proposing that it eventually helps the practitioner to develop what he referred to as *spiritual sight*, as a result of which the unseen spiritual essence of things and of people can be experienced.

Steiner's method differed from the more usual form of direct contemplation in that he used carefully controlled mental processes to augment visual experience. Thus when meditating upon an inanimate object such as a stone, the meditator keeps in the forefront of the mind an awareness of the stone's unchanging form, of its stillness, and of the fact that it is 'not fashioned according to desires, but by power that is devoid of desire'. By contrast, when meditating upon a plant, the meditator remains mentally aware of it as something whose shape changes and develops in accordance with the purpose, the 'desire', of the life force within it (Steiner 1969). Steiner's method thus uses prior awareness to assist the process of direct contemplation, although the meditator must be careful not to allow this awareness to degenerate into mere words. It is a state of mind, rather than a verbal activity.

Self-Observation of Body and Mind

When practising self-observation, direct contemplation is focused upon the self rather than upon external objects. An obvious example is the Buddhist walking meditation known as *kinhin*. In *kinhin*, the meditator typically walks with studied, slow deliberation; each movement of the foot and the legs, each sensation of the sole of the foot touching and lifting from the ground, each subtle change in weight distribution between the left and the right foot, is registered by the mind. The concentration is centred upon the body to the exclusion of distracting thoughts or distracting impressions from the environment. Thus the meditator is in effect looking intently into the act of walking, into the physical actions of the body from moment to moment.

For those of us who live in the City, self-observation can only be as detailed as this for short intervals. But *kinhin* can even be practised as we climb stairs, or as we walk in the garden. Any action can become *kinhin* if we slow it down and focus upon the way in which it unfolds. A bonus is that e learn to be more aware of the body (not in an tical and narcissistic way, but in terms of its use), so we become more aware of the tensions to which we habitually subject it. We notice how the shoulders become hunched, the jaw becomes tight, the neck and the eyes become strained, the hands become clenched, the muscles of the legs and of the lower back tense up. We notice how we put the body under unnecessary strain, how we use more energy than is needed to carry out the simplest of movements, how many of our aches and pains are a direct result of the misuse of groups of muscles, often with one group in conflict with another instead of working together. Practices such as the Alexander Technique or tai chi help greatly in this process of self-observation of the body and its movements.

But self-observation must also be concerned with the mind, and with an increasing ability to recognize why we behave as we do. If we go back to our example of spontaneous kindness, we can begin to recognize what it is in us that allows us from time to time to act in this way, and conversely what prevents us at other times from doing so. We see someone who is in trouble, and we notice a spontaneous impulse in ourselves to come forward and give help. What is it about the plight of the person concerned that touches us? And by contrast, what is it that sometimes holds us back from helping?

Charles Tart insists that to be successful, self-observation must involve a commitment to the truth. We must see what is there, not what we want to be there or what we think ought to be there. We must recognize how our selflessness or selfishness play a part in our actions, how our fear holds us back, how our ability to empathize helps us to come forward. We must notice how the mind tries to 'excuse' us from not helping, how ready we are to turn a blind eye to people's needs, or how much easier it is to offer help if others are watching and approving or if we are attracted to the person we are helping. Conversely, we must recognize what it is that prompts us to give help unselfishly at times, without wishing to draw attention to our actions, and without expecting or wanting anything in return.

Self-observation should also extend to watching how we react to things in general. What is it that pleases and delights us, that excites us and that captures our interest, and why? If this sounds as if it strips all the pleasure from experience, the exact opposite is the case; the more we become able to observe and recognize what is actually happening in our lives, the more we find our true nature within each given experience, and the more we are able to savour the feelings each experience arouses in us. Equally, self-observation should extend to what disconcerts us, or what repels or annoys us. No self-judgement is involved. We simply watch what is going on, and become increasingly aware of each inner response as it arises.

At times we are likely to surprise ourselves by our reactions. We may find that something that usually appeals to us seems curiously flat today, while something which usually leaves us cold is able to strike emotional fire. As we watch ourselves, so we see the inconsistencies in our behaviour, the diversity of our feelings and of our moods, the procession of highs and lows, the boredoms and the search for stimulation, the moments of relaxation and of wellbeing, the energy and the tiredness, the feelings of ease in the presence of some people, and the feelings of tension in the presence of others.

Self-observation also allows us to notice the ideas and feelings we have about ourselves. In counselling, I sometimes listen to people who do not have a good word to say about themselves. It is clear that their inner dialogue is unrelentingly self-critical in a destructive and hurtful way. Like an internalized, disapproving parent or teacher, they sit in judgement upon themselves, constantly discouraging, robbing life of its joy as well as of its spontaneity. On the other hand, I hear people who err on the side of self-indulgence. Their problems are always the result of what other people are doing to them, of the unfairness of the system, of the failure of the world in general to recognize their abilities and to give them the opportunities that they consider they deserve.

Self-Observation and the Emotions

In addition, self-observation enables us to notice the feelings we have about our fellow men and women, the qualities that attract or annoy us about them. As we become more aware of these feelings, so we may find ourselves identifying an important truth about them and about ourselves. Hitherto we may, like most people, have tended to blame our feelings upon others. We think or say things like 'You make me so angry', 'You make me feel so guilty', 'You make me so happy.' But in reality there are no magic buttons on our chests that other people can press in order to 'make' us feel these things. In reality it is not other people who 'do' things to our emotions. Ultimately, it is we who do them to ourselves. Our emotions and our feelings are our own responsibility, and the responsibility of no one else.

This does not imply that we should aim for a rigid control over our emotions. This is the very opposite of the spontaneity we talked about earlier. Extensive control of the emotions indicates that we are frightened (or ashamed) of being who we really are. But it does mean we should be much better at observing our emotions, and at understanding how and why they arise. This allows us, as we grow in self-wisdom, to reach a point where unwanted emotions can be recognized at the very moment they begin to arise, and as a result to lose something of their power over us. Much of this power comes from the fact that we identify so strongly with them. For a few moments we literally *are* our fear or anger, our delight or excitement. This is fine in the case of delight or excitement, but not so helpful in the case of fear or anger. And the truth is that we are not our emotions. If we were, we would only exist when we felt emotional! Self-awareness of exactly what is happening in our emotional life – and why – constitutes the first essential step in dissociating ourselves from the more troublesome elements within it.

What is irritation for example? Someone does or says something of which we disapprove, and we find ourselves in a state described as 'irritated'. What is this state? How do we know we are irritated? What does being irritated feel like? Is it a sensation in the body? If so, where is this sensation? In the arms, the legs, the stomach? Or is it a collection of thoughts? If so, what is the content of these thoughts? Once we have some answers to these questions (and the questions take longer to ask than they need take to answer), the next step is to identify why it is that we have these feelings or these thoughts. What is it about us that has responded in this way to the other person's actions or words?

The answer may have to do with a suspicion that the other person is gaining an unfair advantage over us, or is deliberately trying to annoy us, or is implying that we are no good at our job. Or it may be that we are secretly jealous of their success. Or we could be responding to something about their manner, or about the way they look, or about the way they talk or the way they dress. Whatever it is, it may be less to do with the other person than to do with our own vulnerability or prejudices or readiness to take offence where none is intended.

Once we recognize where our negative emotions are coming from, we can see that it is not the emotions themselves that are the problem, but the way in which we have been using them. All emotions are natural enough, and exist for a purpose, whether it is self-defence or something more constructive. But it is up to us how we use them. It is sometimes suggested to me that the emotions have little to do with spirituality. Nothing could be further from the truth. Spirituality robbed of emotion becomes a cold dry thing, while spirituality controlled by emotion

Techniques of Mindfulness and Self-Observation

The following aids to mindfulness can be practised initially for just a few minutes at a time.

Review of the day.   This is taught by almost all the major spiritual and mystery traditions. Usually carried out before retiring for the night, it consists in mentally recalling as many as possible of the events that have taken place during the previous 24 hours, starting at the point at which the last review ended. Part of this time will have been spent in sleep, so any dreams recalled will form the first part of the review. These should be treated no differently from waking memories. They are events through which one has lived. Then proceed to review what happened during your waking hours. Emotions and feelings are recalled and noted, as well as happenings, conversations and thoughts. Five minutes is initially sufficient for this exercise, and the memories should be run through at an even speed, without dwelling on or judging any of them. As a variant, and as the process of memory improves, the events can be run through in reverse order, starting from the present and running back to the previous review 24 hours earlier.

Visual steadiness.   Our eyes rarely remain still for long. We are constantly scanning our environment, our eyes moving restlessly from one thing to another. The reason for this visual activity is a restless desire for new stimuli. Practise instead visual stillness. Without staring fixedly, or making the exercise too obvious, allow your eyes to rest for longer periods on each object or person before moving away. Take in more detail as you do. If feelings of awkwardness or embarrassment arise, note them and let them go. The same exercise can be practised with sounds or sensations.

Splitting attention. Although, as explained in the text, mindfulness typically involves focusing directly upon whatever it is you are doing, it is valuable, as your powers of mindfulness increase, sometimes to split the attention between two things, remaining equally focused upon both of them. One of the things can be a part of your own body, so that you are aware for example of your left hand while simultaneously focusing upon what you are doing with your right. This exercise not only broadens the field of awareness, it helps remove the feeling that every object, every action, is discrete and separate from every other.

Detailed recall. One of the age-old mindfulness techniques that Rudyard Kipling's young hero Kim was taught was to look for a short time at a tray or table of objects, and then try to recall each of them visually or verbally. This technique soon shows us how little of our environment we habitually take in. Try a modified version of this by recalling the faces of the people on the train during your journey home, or the objects on your desk at work, or the clothes your colleagues were wearing, or the things that were said over lunch or in a meeting during the day.

becomes a thing driven by excesses, whether of blind devotion or of fanatical intolerance. Emotion, and the proper use of emotion, is as important for our spiritual health as it is for our psychological health. Christ defined God as love – ie in terms of the most powerful and the most beautiful emotion known to humankind, rather than in terms of cognitive qualities like intelligence or thinking.

And in trying to describe their experiences, mys
always refer to an awareness of this love, a
overwhelming bliss that comes with it.

It is difficult to self-observe all our negative emotions
during our busy daily lives, so it is often necessary to focus
upon just one of them. For example, we may find ourselves
habitually reacting angrily to the slightest criticism from
colleagues, and trace this back to secret doubts about our
own efficiency, which in turn stem from low self-esteem.
We can therefore set ourselves to observe this reaction, see
it for what it is, and dissociate ourselves from it by not
taking it personally. Either criticism is justified, in which
case it is helpful, or it is unjustified, in which case it should
be ignored.

By practising self-observation, we are able to see deeper
and deeper into our inner lives, and become less and less
the victim of extraneous factors. People sometimes protest
that all this involves a great deal of hard work. So it does,
but laziness is one of the prime enemies on the path of
psychological and spiritual progress. And once we begin to
self-observe, we notice in any case how much energy we
burn up with our tensions, our irritations and our self-
defences. As our powers of mindfulness increase, we notice
that life becomes easier instead of more difficult, that the
days are less tiring and the nights more restful, and that a
profound understanding, felt rather than expressible in
words, begins to inform the way in which we relate to
ourselves and to the outer world.

CHAPTER 8

Who Am I?
I: The Existential Question

The Difficulty of the Question

WE ASSUME WE KNOW who we are. I am David Fontana, and you are Mary Stephens or Paul Williams or Janet Spencer. I am a psychologist and the father of two children, and you are an accountant or a student or a job-seeker, and perhaps also a parent and a householder and a dog-lover and so on. We all of us carry a number of labels which identify us to ourselves and to anyone else who takes an interest in us. So the question 'Who am I?' is easily answered. Or is it? Do these labels indicate who I am or who you, or any of us, really are?

Look at it this way. Your name is something your parents decided to pin upon you, long before you had any say in the matter. Your job and your marital status are roles you play (in the sense that they could conceivably be abolished tomorrow, without abolishing *you*). Your love of dogs and your other likes and dislikes are fluctuating states of mind, sometimes occupying centre stage and at other times pushed into the background by more pressing personal concerns. None of these things can be who you really *are*. Take them all away, and however grievous the loss, you would still be there.

We may therefore be tempted to respond to the question 'Who am I?' with the short answer 'me', and leave it at that. But 'me' is far too general. The 'me' who is happy is very different from the 'me' who is angry, and the 'me' who is

Pondering 'Who Am I?'

Once we begin to ponder the question, and reject all the answers that have to do with our name, profession, family status, sex, age and so on, we realize that the answer must lie much deeper, and that the question itself is a way of asking, 'What is life?' Assuming that there is only one life force behind all existence, rather than a myriad of different life forces, then the answer to the question 'Who am I?' reveals not only our own nature but the nature of all existence. And such an answer must lie beyond words, just as the flavour of jam lies beyond the label on the jar.

If you become bored with the question, extend it by asking 'Who is it who is bored?', and so on. We are born asking questions. Children are full of them, and the wise and caring adult is the one who finds time to listen to these questions, and answer them in a form suitable to the child's understanding, and which does not choke off further questions. The answer 'Of course not' to a question like 'Is there a heaven?' convinces the child that not only is the answer 'no', but that such a question is not even asked by sensible people. On the other hand, the reply 'Why do you want to know?' opens the whole area up for discussion and debate. Zen stresses the need to keep a 'don't know' mind, a mind that is open to direct experience rather than closed by ready-made answers dreamt up by other people.

In a similar way, 'Who am I?' can be allowed to give rise to the reply 'Who wants to know?', and so it goes on. Am I the same person who played games in the garden as a child, who went to university, who made friends, who had relationships, who did this or did that or did the other? Who or what is this mysterious business of being me?

The poet Tennyson found that by repeating his own name over and over again softly to himself he could achieve a state where individual identity disappeared into a mystical experience of unity with all creation. The exercise is very simple. You can use either your first name or your family name. At first, you may find that it is as if someone else is calling you, then memories of the people who have used your name over the years may come back, and your present identity appear to merge with all your past identities. Then there may come a marvellous expansion of oneself, as if one is indeed embracing all things, and the small individuality to which we now cling loses its meaning.

But like all such exercises, this is to be experienced rather than talked about, and your experience may be different from the one I have just described. Have no fear. You *are* real and you *do* exist! The problem is that up to now it is the City that has been telling you (often very confusingly) who you are. It is time to find out for yourself.

angry is very different from the 'me' who is bored/successful/thinking/doing and so on. 'Me' is a portmanteau term which has no real meaning. So perhaps we then decide to break 'me' down into lots of smaller 'me's? But if so, what relationship does each small 'me' have to the portmanteau 'me'? At first, the mind tries to tackle this logically, and answers that each 'me' is linked to all the rest through memory. When 'angry me' is in command, it nevertheless remembers the existence of happy 'me' and of bored 'me', and of every other 'me'. But this makes 'me' no more than a series of memories rather than a contemporary lived experience. In addition, as memory is such a highly fragmented and selective thing, a 'me' built upon it must be a very incomplete sort of entity.

As we continue to question the nature of this 'me', we typically reach a state of not knowing. But another question now arises, 'Who is it who does not know?' There is still somebody (or something) there. Who or what is it? And so the fundamental 'Who am I?' question remains.

The difficulty posed by this question is greatly exacerbated by life in the modern City, which calls upon us to do so many different things at once. During the course of a working day, a woman may have to function variously as a mother, a wife, a taxi driver, a confidant and counsellor, a daughter and a household manager, and this is without the various roles that she will fulfill in her professional career outside the home. A man may have a similarly extensive list of occupations. Often, for both women and men, these various roles clash with each other, producing conflicts of loyalties and pressures of time which add to the difficulties. Amid this welter of demands and confusions, it is little wonder that the question 'Who am I?' is given little real thought.

The Importance of the Question

Yet the question 'Who am I?' is the fundamental existential question whispering away at us each moment of our lives. The American psychologist Ken Wilber (see, for example, Wilber 1983), who has proved so influential in tracing the links between psychology and spirituality, writes that the attempt to answer this question has in fact 'always been held to be the basic path, perhaps the sole path', underlying all the great spiritual traditions. If we know the answer to this question, we quite literally know the answer to all other existential enquiries. We know what (if anything) we were before birth, we know what (if anything) is the purpose of living, we know what (if anything) happens to us after death, we know what (or who) is responsible for our creation, and for the external world that composes the phenomenal field within which we live and move and have our being.

Such an answer does not come easily. In fact we probably have to be fully enlightened before we know it fully. But once we recognize that this is the question that underlies all our other questions on the spiritual path, we have no difficulty in realizing that the answer does not lie in any of the labels we have acquired over the years. We know that behind all the roles and demands that seem to define our lives for us, there is a reality that transcends them all, and is untouched by them, a reality that little by little reveals itself as we go on asking the question.

Knowledge of who we are is quite different from knowing the facts of human biochemistry and the other details that make up the so-called life sciences. It is quite different from knowing the theories of sub-atomic physics and the energy systems that constitute matter. It is quite different from knowing the facts of evolution, of genetics, and of our own personal life history. It is quite different even from knowing about the doctrines and dogmas of the great religions of the world. In short, it is not 'knowing about' anything at all. If we can usefully refer to it in words, we can say that it is a special kind of experience, rather than a set of formulae or descriptions. We can only *experience* who we are, knowing it by being it, and such knowing can only happen when we have stripped away all the irrelevant ideas and notions about ourselves behind which we have learnt – or been taught – to hide.

Not for nothing did the Buddha refuse to answer questions about the ultimate state of being. Great teachers like the Buddha are less concerned with dogma and doctrine than with encouraging a certain activity of mind. We find this activity pared to its bare bones in Zen. The Zen method (particularly in its use of the koan – see Chapter 6) could be said to reduce to the one word 'Who?' (or 'Why?', another way of asking the same thing). One explores this word with *great faith* (unyielding confidence that there is an answer), *great determination* (unshakeable resolution to find that answer), and *great doubt* (unwavering refusal to accept anything less than that answer). 'Even when you are not asking the question in words,' the Chinese Ch'an Master Sheng Yen once instructed me, 'keep the wordless enquiry in your mind.' As if, in fact, the energy to ask the question is always there, poised and expectant. But beware the rational mind, with its readiness to offer elegant yet empty solutions!

Zen's Approach to an Answer

'Keep the question "Who?" like something sweet in the mouth,' Sheng Yen taught me, an all-embracing 'Who?' that even includes the question itself, and which is an aspect of what in Zen is termed the 'don't know mind'. A 'don't know mind' takes the seeker beyond answers in words, and brings him or her to sudden moments of realization when, fleetingly but unmistakably, the first glimpse of the answer appears. These moments are referred to by Zen teachers as an experience of the suchness of things, which is at one and the same time a realization of their ordinariness and of their profound and unforgettable extraordinariness.

In that moment of suchness, the barrier between one's own mind and the rest of creation disappears. If we want to dress this up in philosophical language, we can say that one experiences the fact that the phenomenal world is a creation of the mind, and that everything is happening inside this mind – or rather that the play of the mind is infinite and encompasses everything. But it is much more even than this. It is a realization that there is no distinction between the play of the mind and the sights and sounds that go to make up this play.

The Sūraṅgama Sutra (quoted in Luk 1971) puts it thus:

Your body and mind as well as external mountains,
Rivers, space and the great Earth are but phenomena
Within the wondrous bright True Mind.

The Zen approach is particularly suited to those of us who
live in the City. This is because the suchness of things is
simply the reality of things as they are. When Zen masters
are asked the question 'What is Zen?' they reply with such
things as 'Your ordinary everyday life', 'Chopping wood,
drawing water', 'Joy in the morning, sleep at night, what
else?' Zen is simply what is, once you stop being deceived
by it. Zen is 'direct pointing at reality', a way of seeing and
acting that comes from who you really are rather than from
who you think you are. Zen is not withdrawal from the
City into some remote monastery (though Zen monasteries
do exist), but an active engagement with life that refuses to
mistake words and definitions and descriptions for the real
business of being alive.

Zen also reminds us that as we fulfil our many roles in
the City, the 'Who am I?' question should never be far from
our minds. It is a wonderful way of reminding ourselves
when we have deserted the spiritual path and assumed a
role which is foreign to it. The problems related to our
occupation in the workplace are dealt with more fully in
Chapter 12, but during the working day we may find
ourselves filling a role which calls upon us to deceive
others or to take advantage of their weakness. The answer
to the question 'Who am I?' is that, in that moment, we
have become a deceiver or someone who exploits the
vulnerabilities of others.

Self-observation of this kind is not a recipe for perpetual
guilt. We are not perfect human beings, but simply men
and women trying to do our best. Self-observation is not
like having a judge sitting always on our shoulders. It is a
way of preventing us from deluding ourselves about the
progress we have made, and a way of indicating where
more work is needed. We may think we are advanced

Imagination and Visualization

As it is our minds that co-create the appearance of the visible world (including our own bodies) from the energy field which is its root cause, it makes sense that by changing the way in which we perceive the world, we can bring about deep changes in ourselves and our relationship to it. Spiritual and mystery traditions have been saying this for centuries, and modern research into the mind-body link in illness and in health is beginning to demonstrate that they are right.

The key lies in imagination, the importance of which was stressed in Chapter 4. Let us take the body as our example. If we use our imagination to visualize something about our body as being different from what it is, then this visualization appears capable of instigating a change in the psychological or physical energies associated with it. In Tantric Buddhism, for example, the meditator is taught to visualize the Buddha, in minute detail, sitting opposite. At the end of the meditation, the Buddha is visualized as merging into the meditator, and thus as conferring upon the him or her the qualities of a Buddha. The result is that the meditator releases his or her dormant potential for these qualities within the self. An alternative practice actually has the meditator visualizing *becoming* the Buddha.

In psychotherapy and hypnotherapy we sometimes ask clients to imagine themselves possessing qualities needed for psychological growth (self-confidence, courage, tenderness etc), and results show that, provided the client's imagination is good enough, psychological change can take place. In medicine, the visualization of oneself as whole and well again, or as fighting off infection or cancer cells, can also help produce healing (see, for example, Epstein 1989, Simonton and others 1980).

If we think of the body as made of solid material, and the mind as simply electrical and chemical processes within the brain, all this seems impossibly far-fetched. But if we think of the body as a constantly changing and flowing set of interactive energy systems, things look very different. The way in which we think profoundly influences how we see material reality, and what we can and cannot do with that reality.

Another example can be taken from sports psychology (Gallwey 1986). Athletes are taught over and over again to visualize themselves as winning the race or as clearing the high jump, and to *feel* all the elation of success. The golfer is taught to visualize the flight of the golf ball, the diver to perform the perfect dive, the darts thrower to hit the exact spot on the board and so on. These various processes – spiritual development, healing the body, success at sport – may all seem very different, but the principle behind them is the same. By imagining an achievement in as much detail as we can, we render ourselves more likely to attain that achievement. The lesson involved in all this will not escape the City dweller.

practitioners, and then we catch ourselves refusing a reasonable request from a child or a colleague because we cannot be bothered, or find ourselves overcome by jealousy, envy, resentment or pettiness over something or other. In such moments our conscious identity is that of someone who cannot be bothered, or of someone who is jealous, envious, resentful or petty. It is certainly not that of an advanced practitioner!

To practise Zen does not mean that one must first become

a Buddhist. Thomas Merton, the Cistercian monk who had a deep understanding of Zen from a Christian perspective and who wrote widely on the subject, puts it thus (Merton 1976): 'Zen points directly to being itself, without indulging in speculation.' It is the practice beyond all practices, the essence of any and all spiritual paths. A more recent Christian exponent of Zen is the Jesuit Hugo Enomiya-Lassalle (1990), while the unrivalled interpreter of Christianity from a Zen perspective was the great Japanese scholar and practitioner D. T. Suzuki (eg 1979). Both men emphasize that Zen is a way of living, a way of practising the spiritual path, and not a dogmatic belief or doctrine.

Modern Science's Approach to an Answer

Living as we do in the City, we are constantly brought up against modern science. We not only see its effects all around us, and make use of its discoveries 24 hours of the day, we are also surrounded on all sides by scientific ideas and scientific ways of thinking. We learn them in school, we absorb them from the media, we study and apply them in professional life. Living a spiritual life in the City, we find all too often that science seems to propose a world-view so different from our own that it seems the two cannot exist together (see Chapter 2).

The hard-nosed, materialist-reductionist philosophy espoused by many scientists appears to leave no room for non-material realities such as a soul or a spirit, or even a mind. In answer to the question 'Who am I?' they would answer in terms of chemistry, biology and physics. No one can effectively follow the spiritual path in the City without wishing to resolve the apparent conflict between science and religion. Yet like so many things that are polarized by words and arguments, the conflict between science and spirituality is more apparent than real, sustained by scientists and religionists who have no real owledge of each other's point of view.

We can see this if we look at the words quoted earlier from the Sūraṅgama Sutra in the light of modern physics. Far from retaining its erstwhile materialist-reductionist stance, physics now tells us that, instead of being composed of hard, solid, static objects, all matter is in fact a constant flow of energy. Atoms, instead of being the building blocks of matter as was once thought, are almost entirely empty space, and the minute proportion that is not empty space consists of mysterious particles which are not 'things' in the accepted sense of the word at all, but wave forms or vibrations – though what, if anything, is waving or vibrating remains a mystery.

In practical terms, this means that the phenomenal world, the familiar world 'out there' of trees and houses and cars and butterflies, is not what it seems. Goodness knows what it really is. An approximation would be to say that it is a whirling flux of energy, but even that begs the question of what this energy actually is. One thing seems fairly certain. The familiar world in front of you and me is actually called into being by our act of experiencing it. When you go out of the room and close the door behind you, the room literally ceases to exist in the form in which you have just seen it. So does whatever you are looking at or listening to this very moment should you stop looking at or listening to it.

Thus a better scientific answer to the 'Who am I?' question is that we are in a real sense the co-creators of the visible world. Its dazzling beauty is a combination of the primal flux of energy 'out there', and the way in which our senses and our minds are programmed to experience this flux. And since our bodies are made of the same material as the rest of the world, this applies just as much to our physical forms (ie to the energy fields which you and I both inhabit) as it does to everything else. It is thus true for the scientist to say, with the Sutra, that all things in the world 'out there' are really phenomena within the mind. The

answer to the question 'Who am I', whether given by the
scientist or the spiritual seeker, must therefore encompass
this truth. The difference is that for the scientist the answer
remains a formula within the head, while for the spiritual
seeker it is a living and ultimately a lived experience.

CHAPTER 9

Who Am I?
II: A Glimpse of the
Enlightened Mind

What Is Enlightenment?

WHY SHOULD THE direct experience of our oneness with the rest of creation referred to in the last chapter lead to those ineffable states described (as best they can) by those who have actually experienced them? One of the major causes of human misery, felt particularly keenly in the City, is a feeling of alienation, of being cut off emotionally and physically from our fellow men and women, of being unloved and perhaps unlovable. As a psychologist I see this time after time in the people who come to me for help. By contrast, one of the major causes of human happiness is the feeling that one loves and is loved, that one is part of a relationship or a community that extends one's individuality and allows one to feel greater than the small, limited self. Now take this feeling of being loved and multiply it by as many thousands as you care to imagine. This, then, is something of the experience of enlightenment, an experience that leaves one *knowing* that the reality behind all existence is love, and that one is not just loved but an inseparable part of this love.

As this feeling embraces not just what exists in the small present moment, but the whole of creation from the unimaginable past to the unforeseeable future, it brings with it the certainty of one's own eternal nature. The life force that runs within us and inhabits this energy field that

we call the body was, is and ever will be transcend:
overarching the individuality of the moment, bui
losing itself in an impersonal sea because reality includes
both the individuality that experiences the whole, and the
whole that experiences the individuality.

Thus enlightenment experiences bring with them feelings of indescribable serenity and bliss. Those who have
experienced them no longer just believe that men and
women are more than their material selves, they actually
and actively *know* this to be the case. Even a momentary
glimpse of the enlightened state is enough to convey this
certainty. As we saw from the story of Han Shan (Chapter
1), even advanced souls rarely remain permanently in the
enlightened state. Enlightenment comes and goes,
glimpsed momentarily like a beacon on a distant hill before
being obscured again by the mists of our own chattering,
distracting minds. But once it is glimpsed, from however
far away, we know it is there and our feet are pointing in
the right direction.

How, I am sometimes asked, do we know if someone else
is enlightened (or, more realistically, has experienced
significant enlightenment experiences)? Teachers appear
from time to time who claim to be permanently in this state.
My own experience is that the louder their claims, the less
likely they are to be true, and this issue is returned to in
Chapter 15. I have, as far as I can judge, only worked
closely with three enlightened people in this life, a rare
privilege for which I feel humbly grateful. Two were Indian
holy women, and the third a Chinese Ch'an master.
Outwardly very different, they left me with the same
abiding feeling, a feeling which I have tried many times to
put into words. The nearest I come to it is that in the
presence of these three people I realized I had nothing, and
could have nothing, to give them. I was aware that everything that could be given was already being given to *me*, in
the form of unconditional love, an all-powerful compassion
which contained nothing of self. Yet paradoxically,

although the love was given impersonally, it contained something that was intensely personal. It came from a boundless source, yet it knew me and loved me better than I knew and loved myself.

When I say that I had nothing to give them, what I mean is that, not with my mind but with my heart, I knew myself to be in the presence of beings without ego. If there is no ego, there is nothing one wants for oneself, because in a sense everything is already there. One is free from the artificial prison, constructed for us by others in our childhood and laboriously added to by our own hands over the years, of who we think we are. Therefore there was no need of gratitude, of gifts, of adulation. It is only the ego that craves these things, and wants always to grasp the material sweets of existence.

Certainly any encounter with a spiritually advanced teacher leaves one with the realization that there is so much one needs to give, but the giving is for the benefit of one's own development, and has to do with letting go of unnecessary burdens rather than with satisfying any need in the teacher. A need implies a deficiency, and the deficiencies are in oneself and not in the teacher.

It is sometimes said that the very act of meeting a spiritually advanced teacher can lead to a deep inner transformation and to rapid subsequent progress on the spiritual path. In other words, that the teacher can do much of the work for you. It is more accurate to say that meeting the teacher, provided you are in the right frame of mind at the time, allows a shift in your level of consciousness, not unlike the shift that takes place in response to great art or music. No words need be spoken. In fact, words can sometimes be a hindrance. When sitting meditating in the company of a holy man or woman, the silence is so total that it seems like an extra presence in the room. The Sanskrit term for sitting with the master (as I have said, I use the term 'master' here to stand for both male and male teachers) in this way is *darshan*, which literally

means not only a splendid sight, but also inner understanding. Thus while contemplating the master outwardly,
the meditator is also contemplating him- or herself inward-
ly, and seeing there the spiritual qualities exemplified by
the master.

It is possible that a single experience of *darshan* can help
to bring about a permanent transformation in the way in
which you experience yourself, but for most of us, it is
more a matter of being shown the way to the goal than of
actually being transported there. We have, as all the great
traditions teach, to accept some of the responsibility for
ourselves. There is certainly a gift of grace during *darshan*,
a gift which arrives unexpectedly and surprises us with joy,
producing a sudden elevation of the spirits, as if the body
has become light and transparent, and the very self has
dissolved into the certainty of being loved and cared for.
But even in *darshan* such moments only happen to those
who are prepared for them, and who have desired them
and awaited them with patience.

Self-Actualization

In the City we rarely – perhaps never – have the chance to
sit in *darshan* with enlightened men and women. But
darshan happens even in the presence of people who make
no pretence to being spiritual masters. Our spirits rise
automatically when we are with such people, no matter
how quiet and unassuming they are. Whether we meet
them socially or in the workplace they have a life-
enhancing quality which touches all who are open to it, and
leaves us feeling in some intangible way better about
ourselves, more at ease, more confident of our worth, more
prepared to tackle the demands of daily life. If not
enlightened, we have the feeling that such people are
certainly on their way towards this state.

Men and women who have this life-enhancing quality

often listen more than they talk. They have an interest in their fellows which has nothing to do with idle curiosity; they never seek to put them down, or to impress them or assume superiority over them. When they do talk, they invariably have something interesting or telling to say. Although active and effective in the world and in their use of time, they typically have a quality of inner peace and repose, and appear to observe and learn from the world rather than lose themselves in chatter or misdirected endeavours. There is no compulsion about their behaviour; rather they seem free to choose their path through life or, if prevented from doing so, free to choose to accept what life brings.

They talk little about themselves, although they answer personal questions honestly and openly when asked. They seem to have a deep store of wisdom to which they refer when others seek their guidance or advice. They rarely push themselves forward, but are usually on hand when needed. Typically they refuse to resort to dogma or doctrines learnt from others, but relate more to direct experience, and to a deep sense of humanity and compassion. Often they have the gift of beautifying their physical environment, not through wealth or ostentation but through a natural creativity which allows them to recognize and use simple things in novel and harmonious ways.

Abraham Maslow, one of the founders of humanistic psychology (a movement within psychology designed to study the whole person rather than isolated fragments of behaviour), referred to such people as 'self-actualized', that is as having developed and used themselves in accordance with their true potential as human beings, and in consequence as manifesting genuine psychological health. His research with a sample of people (all of whom lived and worked in the City) regarded by their peers as having self-actualized qualities identified them as:

perceptive, emotionally open, natural and spontaneous, problem-centred in their approach (as opposed to self-centred), happy with their own company, autonomous (ie independent rather than under the control of events or of other people), accepting of self and others (as opposed to being over-critical and judgemental), appeciative of life, capable of deep relationships with loved ones, and humourous, creative, ethical, goal-orientated, democratic, and consistent.

If this makes them sound like impossible paragons of virtue, be reassured. Maslow found that they also have imperfections, some of which arise from their very strengths. For example their independence and goal-orientation can make them seem ruthless or anti-social at times, while their compassion can lead them to become too closely involved with neurotic and over-demanding people. They are also by no means free of the guilt, anxieties, sadness, self-blame, internal strife and conflict suffered by the rest of the human race, but the difference is that in their case these states of mind do not stem from neurotic sources. They are related to realistic appraisals of life events rather than to imaginary or exaggerated problems, and are not allowed to dominate thinking, to become obsessional, or to interfere with personal effectiveness.

Maslow also noted that self-actualized people usually report experiencing what he called 'peak experiences', that is moments of ecstasy, wonder and awe when they feel themselves to be outside time and space, experiencing limitless horizons and the certainty that something transforming and extraordinary has happened which lends strength even to everyday life. Such moments seem akin to mystical and enlightenment experiences, and are often associated with spiritual or philosophical insights, with artistic enjoyment or inspiration, and with the feelings of self-transcendence and universal unity and love which I have already spoken about.

Most of the self-actualizers identified by Maslow were more than usually successful in their professional lives, but

Self-Actualized People

The people identified by Maslow as self-actualized come from all walks of life. Many public figures are among them, some historical (selected because of their work and the accounts given of them by their contemporaries), some modern. Among Maslow's examples of self-actualizers were Albert Einstein, Eleanor Roosevelt (wife of American President Franklin D Roosevelt), William James (eminent philosopher and one of the founding fathers of modern psychology), Albert Schweitzer (medical doctor, musician and missionary), Aldous Huxley (writer, mystic, and interpreter of Eastern spiritual thought), and Benedict Spinoza (17th-century philosopher who emphasized that God is immanent in all created things).

Others selected as having many self-actualizing qualities were the German playwright Johann Goethe, the cellist Pablo Casals, the theologian Martin Buber, the poets John Keats, Robert Browning, Ralph Waldo Emerson, Henry Longfellow and Walt Whitman, the American politician Adlai Stevenson, George Washington, the composer Joseph Haydn, the Irish writer and mystic George William Russell (pen-name A E), and the great American diplomat and writer Benjamin Franklin.

We can add names of our own choosing to these lists. The Dalai Lama comes immediately to mind, as does the musician Yehudi Menuhin, and the people named in connection with the various yogas in Chapter 3: Mother Teresa, Krishnamurti, Sai Baba (whom many would place above mere mortals) and B K Iyengar; and there are other holy men and women who also qualify.

d your own examples. You may find precious Why? Why is it that so many public figures (politicians, sportspeople, media 'personalities' etc) fail to show self-actualizing qualities? Is it because of the decay in those spiritual values that regard us as more than physical bodies, and that prize the inner life and selfless compassion? Is it because of the modern, pervasive scientific philosophy that holds that we are biological accidents, motivated by little more than selfish genes and self-gratification?

Where has the City gone wrong, that it values currency speculators, pop stars, politicians and advertising executives above those who care for the sick and the weak, and who educate the young? Living a spiritual life means that we must constantly re-examine the City's values and our own. It is not an easy option, but one upon which the survival of our species may depend. For our future depends upon self-actualized people and the transmission of self-actualizing values to our children and our fellows. Even the possession of a few of these values is confirmation that the individuals concerned recognize and attempt to follow the spiritual path.

their professions were not necessarily high-profile ones. One of the most conspicuously self-actualized people known to me began his career as an army officer, but gave it up in order to become a jobbing farmhand, which means that he goes where the seasonal work takes him, working long hours during busy times such as lambing and harvesting, and at other times doing routine and repair jobs as they become available. He also writes and publishes poetry in his spare time, and takes parties of people to Ladakh and Tibet and other remote places, leading always by example, showing great physical and psychological courage, and at the same time great compassion and concern. Whatever the task on which he is engaged, from splitting logs and mending farm gates to composing poetry or studying life in Himalayan villages, he brings the same concentration and dignity to bear, honouring the task and being honoured in turn by it.

Finding the Self

We can sum all this up by saying that self-actualized people seem profoundly aware that life consists of more than the limited self, and that the boundaries between this self and the rest of creation are illusory. In almost all cases, they are also conscious that 'the rest of creation' includes deep and unfathomable mysteries into which the limited self merges in some mystical yet ultimately knowable way.

Of course, the problem for those who live in the City is often not the rather grand one of how to go beyond the limited self, but the more mundane one of finding and asserting any kind of self in the first place. An American colleague once put it to me that many people have to work desperately hard to hold their fragmented personalities together, and 'pretend to be whole people'. What he meant was that they are so buffeted by the competitive, aggressive environment of the City, and by the self-doubt and self-rejection that the City induces, that the question 'Who am I?' can only be tackled by them at the most basic level. Instead of using their energies for personal growth and the development of enriching relationships with the outside world, all their efforts are spent in trying to survive. In consequence, elevated talk about moving beyond the self and achieving higher states of realization carries little meaning for them.

It is quite true that people in this position need first to 'find' and assert the self in order to be able to lose it. The well-known Indian teacher Bhagwan Shree Rajneesh used to put it that you should 'give God your ego, but make sure it is a good ego'. Before the ego is 'good' (ie sufficiently strong), the thought of trying to go beyond it can be a terrifying one. A useful analogy can be drawn from the behaviour of very young children. We know that such children show far more interest in exploring their environment and finding out about life if they know that they have a secure base in the form of loving, supportive parents or caregivers to which they can return. Children who are unsure of the love and protection of their parents and caregivers have no such security, and show far more timidity and clinging behaviour as a result. They are less ready to set out on voyages of discovery, far more likely to experience anxiety in the presence of the unknown, and much less confident about their ability to cope with and to enjoy life.

Psychological and spiritual progress seems to depend therefore upon first building the secure base of a clear and confident personal identity, in which each aspect of the self is in harmony with all other aspects. Only when this is done is one strong enough to transcend the self in order to find out what lies beyond. Progress depends upon first learning to be oneself, and then recognizing that as this 'self' is largely a superficial construction, it cannot be the primary essence, the *materia prima* as the medieval alchemists called it, from which our conscious existence springs. Once this recognition has taken place, there comes a longing to know this primary essence. Christianity refers to it as the urge to seek the Kingdom of Heaven, Hinduism talks of the need to find the Self, while Buddhism speaks of the wish to experience the Buddha Nature.

One problem we have in the City is that all too often our education (both formal in schools, and informal at home) forces us to do things the other way around. In childhood, social and cultural constraints constantly prevent children from learning to be – and to assert – themselves. The child has to conform to patterns laid down by adults, and to live up to the expectations of others. Self-assertion in children is all too often interpreted as insolence or insubordination, and is suppressed rather than identified and understood. In adulthood, by contrast, the prizes go to those who *can* assert themselves. In business, in politics, in the academic world, it is the self-assertive person who is most valued and most rewarded. And where self-assertion is frustrated, the result is all too often either a damaging acceptance of personal inadequacy or an urge to compensate by scape-goating those weaker than oneself such as minorities, young children, domestic partners and animals.

As a consequence of these educational pressures, we all too often find ourselves going against the natural flow of our own development. Frustrated, misunderstood, and often alienated from ourselves in childhood, we try in adult life to win ourselves back, but often at the cost of losing yet more of the authentic individual our human potential actually intended us to be.

Who Am I?: An Agenda for Action

This is why the question 'Who am I?' is of such enormous value. Whether in the process of learning how to assert the limited self or of moving beyond it, the question allows us to be more objective about ourselves. The answers that arise are appropriate to where we happen to be at the moment. 'Who am I?', once we have worked through the most obvious labels mentioned in the last chapter, soon takes us into progressively deeper levels of the personality. Answers such as 'I am a parent' lead to questions such as 'What is a parent?', which in turn become 'Am I a parent (in the full sense of the word)?' One does not have consciously to ask these deeper questions. The basic query remains 'Who am I?' It is simply that as the question probes deeper and deeper into us other questions arise of themselves, often as a set of feelings rather than as a form of words.

The busy life of the City has hitherto left us no space – and no method – for self-enquiry. But the question 'Who am I?', at once the simplest and most profound of all questions, now provides us with both. Answers such as 'I am a man', or 'I am a woman' take us into the meaning of maleness and femaleness, and the qualities that go with being a man or a woman; then as we go deeper, we go beyond maleness and femaleness and become a human being – and what does being a human being mean?

We cannot and must not try and force this questioning or attempt to short-circuit it (for example by plunging in with a question about being a human being before we have dealt with the maleness and femaleness which feature far more prominently in our everyday identity). This would be artificial and sterile, like presenting children with misleading answers to questions they have not yet even learnt to ask. Instead, we should proceed naturally to each level of the question when – and only when – the previous level has been reached and resolved. Thus the self is allowed to assert itself, and to recognize its weaknesses and its strengths, the areas where more work needs to be done (and what form this work should take), and the areas that have hitherto been neglected or undervalued, or passed over without notice.

As we grow in self-understanding, so we find that we grow in self-acceptance, and then in self-love (which is not the same thing as growing in conceit or falling 'in love' with ourselves). We are as we are, part of the suchness of things, a continually evolving and developing stream of the life force. It is up to us to see that this evolution and development take us in the right direction, but we are as much a part of this force as everyone else, and as much a part of the love which is its essence.

Although the question 'Who am I?' is asked continually, there is nothing relentless about it. We are not in front of the inquisition. We have enough problems deali insatiable demands of the City, without laying burden upon ourselves. Instead, the questic played with, in the way that we play w absorbing, intriguing puzzle. As Sheng Yen advised me, it should be held 'like sweetness in the mouth'. At the same time, we must never allow it to degenerate into mere habit. Remember the Zen injunction to proceed with great faith, great determination and great doubt.

The answers to the question 'Who am I?' sketch out, at each level, an agenda for action. They prompt us to see where we are, and what needs to be done if we are to integrate and use the self, and then to search for what lies beyond. The question takes us across the barrier that must be surmounted between conscious and unconscious, so that we cease to be strangers to ourselves and can move more freely and effectively through our inner world. And the answers give us the ability to move more freely and effectively through the City, coping with its challenges and its rewards and disappointments. Maslow's self-actualized people have realized many of these answers in their own lives, and it is useful from time to time to reread the qualities that he identified in them, not because we should try and force these qualities upon ourselves, but because each of them is already there within us, ready to emerge once the the question has penetrated to its level.

CHAPTER 10

Pilgrimages and Retreats

DON JUAN, the Yaqui Indian portrayed in Carlos Castaneda's books on shamanic beliefs and practices (most recently 1993), is reported as saying that those who live in the everyday world but follow the path of inner spiritual development must live 'a life of *controlled folly*'. One way of interpreting this is that although aware of the temporary, insubstantial nature of many of the material things we have to do, and of the folly that characterizes much of our modern, artificial way of life, we must nevertheless operate within the everyday world *as if* we take it seriously. Guidance of this kind is highly relevant for those of us who live in the City. It reminds us that we should not mistake the City for ultimate reality and put all our efforts into material aggrandizement and pleasures, but nor should we waste time wringing our hands over the world that people have made for themselves, or in wishing we could turn our backs upon it and become hermits. We have to live usefully and effectively in the world, relating to it as it is, and contributing to its betterment and to the welfare of others.

Relating to the world as it is does not mean, however, that temporary withdrawal is wrong. In fact such withdrawal is essential in order to find the peace and silence necessary for inner growth. Those who live in the City must make space in their lives for this peace and silence, no matter how pressing the demands of the world happen to be. There are several ways in which this can be done. One is through the practices of meditation and of mindfulness, as described in Chapters 6 and 7. Other ways are through pilgrimages, retreats, and, strange as it may at first sight seem, through paying proper attention to our nightly excursions into the dream world. Retreats and pilgrimages are dealt with in this chapter, while dreams are covered in the next.

Pilgrimage

'Pilgrimage' sounds a grand term, but with a certain attitude of mind any journey can be a pilgrimage, and I would love to see the word brought back into more general – and practical – use, for we need a term to describe an activity as important to the modern City dweller as it was to pious men and women in the Middle Ages. Making a pilgrimage need not involve going to a recognized pilgrim centre. Certainly there are sites which have particular spiritual power. For example there are the great cathedrals of Europe such as Canterbury in Britain, St Peter's in Rome and Santiago de Compostela in Spain, each a centre of medieval pilgrimage. And there are many non-Christian sites such as the shrine of the God Apollo at Delphi in Greece, which stands in a majestic sweep of hillside facing the early morning sun, the great pyramid of Giza in Egypt, and the temples of the Upper Nile.

Then there are the temples of India, some of them with carved stonework delicate as lace, and the great pyramids of the Mayan Indians in Mexico brooding on hidden mysteries and forgotten gods, and the ancient monoliths and standing stones of northern Europe laid out with a precise geometry that still invites the awe of modern man (read about them for example in John Mitchell's marvellously evocative *New View Over Atlantis*). But all these great centres of worship are hallowed not by the presence of bishops and priests or even the bones of the saints buried

there, but by the faith of the countless thoi
folk who have been drawn to them over th
who have visited them not as tourists but as seei.
some truth about themselves and their relationship wiu.
the unseen world.

In all pilgrimages, I repeat, it is the attitude of mind that
counts. Any journey carried out in the service of one's
spiritual nature is a pilgrimage. There may not even be a
specific destination in view (medieval pilgrims referred to
such goalless journeys as 'peregrinations', and embarked
upon them to 'seek the Lord we know not whither'). And
where a specific destination exists, the pilgrim should not
travel towards it with a preconceived notion of what will be
found there. An open, receptive mind gains more benefit
than one bent upon imposing its own expectations upon
experience. Sometimes one is not aware that anything of
value has happened until afterwards, even long afterwards.
It is as if the pilgrimage sowed a seed, which needed time
to germinate before coming to flower.

The attitude of mind should therefore be one of not
knowing rather than of knowing, the 'not knowing' of a
small child, who approaches each fresh experience with
wonder, engaging in it with a spontaneous directness free
of anticipation. In adult life our heads are crammed so full
of ideas about the world and ourselves that we fall into the
habit of defining, explaining and judging experience
without giving it a chance to speak for itself. This is fine –
even necessary – in its place, but a pilgrimage is an
opportunity to shift our consciousness back to a mode of
not defining, not explaining and not judging.

Going on pilgrimage is like going to a well. Who knows
how deep the water will be, or how it will taste, or how
much we can bring back with us? No matter what we
discover, we are likely to be changed as a result. Sometimes
the change brings a sense of delight, or of a new inner
harmony, or of a fresh understanding. But at other times it
may bring a sense of puzzled unease, as if it has revealed

new uncertainties, or a glimpse of richer possibilities which awaken fresh discontent with life in the City. Such lessons, although uncomfortable at the time, can be particularly valuable in that they are a major incentive to continue and deepen our spritual practice. In *The Journey of the Magi*, the poet T S Eliot perfectly expresses this unease through the reflections of one of the magi, back in his own country after journeying to the birthplace of Christ (Eliot 1974).

> We returned to our places, these Kingdoms,
> But no longer at ease here, in the old dispensation,
> With an alien people clutching their gods.

Pilgrimages in the City

Often a pilgrimage can be built into a day or days within an ordinary holiday. But whenever or wherever it takes place, it is best to travel as lightly as possible, carrying only essentials. Unnecessary lumber clutters the mind as well as the body. Our forebears took very little with them, even when they set out for what in those days amounted to vast journeys across land or sea. The more we need possessions to satisfy our wants or to lend us security, the less we allow ourselves to be in contact with our own inner resources.

With the right attitude of mind, a walk in the country, even a walk through the streets of the City, can become a pilgrimage, bringing moments of illumination in which the sense of one's relationship to the rest of existence suddenly stands out with startling and unexpected clarity. Some City dwellers transform a favourite walk into a daily pilgrimage. Others have a quiet park to which they go, or a churchyard, or even a much-loved tree in a small back garden. In each case these brief pilgrimages provide a priceless moment in which the mind returns to itself, and escaping from the world of man-made objects, experiences once more its oneness with the natural order.

Pilgrimages of the Mind

At times when it is difficult or impossible to get away on a physical pilgrimage, the journey can be carried out in the landscape of the mind. This may involve recalling (in as much detail as possible) a previous pilgrimage. Or it may entail a pilgrimage that you would like to make, to a specific place at a specific time of year. But it can also be entirely imaginary, with the unconscious supplying the details, much as it does in dreams or in creative work.

You can decide on the form of your own imaginary pilgrimage (and remember before you start not to debate whether your experiences are 'real' or not). Or you can use the format given below. Either way, once you have set the scene, allow the unconscious to do the work for you. The more this happens, the deeper you are going into yourself.

- Sit in a comfortable, alert posture, as if in meditation. Focus first upon the breathing (Chapter 6), and allow the mind to settle into a clear and relaxed state. Now visualize a white five-barred gate, set in a fence or a wall, with a view of open country beyond, and a path winding into the distance. Do not hurry. Allow the visualization to build itself up, and allow yourself time to take in the details. If the visualization is not very clear, do not worry. Stay with whatever is there.

- Now walk forward into the visualization, push open the gate and step through onto the path. Although there is no need to look around, keep the impression that the visualization extends behind you and to either side as well as in front. Begin to walk, feeling the path beneath your feet, and the wind or the sun on your face. Notice the sky and the landscape.

- When you have gone a little way, look down at yourself. What are you wearing? What are you carrying? (There are no right and wrong answers; just look.)

- Allow the journey to take as long as it needs, but have in your mind the knowledge that the path is leading you to a definite place. Perhaps around the next bend, or at the summit of the next hill, you will see your destination in the distance.

- Allow the destination to appear in its own time, and to be itself. Do not try to decide in advance what it will be. Do not be surprised, disappointed or overjoyed by whatever you see. It is itself, nothing more, nothing less.

- Enter your destination.

At the close of the pilgrimage, retrace your steps (this is important, though it can be done more quickly than the outward journey), go through the five-barred gate, and imagine yourself turning around and sitting once more in meditation.

No matter how vivid the experiences one meets on a pilgrimage, whether it is to a great cathedral or the shade of a tree in the back garden, the problem is how to retain the insights involved, the mystical awareness of a transformed mind, when one becomes reabsorbed into the mundane realities of the City. All too frequently the memory starts to fade, the moment of clarity to appear no more than a dream, and a sense of loss and disillusionment invades the spirit. The rational mind begins to make 'sense' of the experience, denying its validity and relegating it to the lumber-room of wishful thinking or of overactive imagination. But the golden touchstone which must never be lost is the knowledge that you are simply observing the natural activity of mind. It is in the nature of mind that memories dim as the days go past. And it is in the nature of mind (certainly of the conditioned Western mind) that in the misplaced rationality of hindsight we doubt experiences that lie outside the boundaries of normal explanation, however convinced we were of their reality at the time.

It would be nice to think that 'enlightenment' brings with it a complete and permanent reorientation of our inner being, so that we can never slip back into the old doubts and uncertainties. But remember, once again, the example of Han Shan in Chapter 1. Like Han Shan, we go through many enlightenment experiences rather than a once and for all transformation. Even the Buddha spent many years on the path before he reached ultimate enlightenment during his many days of continuous meditation under the boh tree at Bodh Gaya. There *may* be individuals who are enlightened fully and finally at a stroke, but I have my doubts. The only people I have met who have claimed such exalted experiences have left me with grave doubts as to whether they have sighted even the first of the many doors leading in that direction.

Retreat

The distinction between pilgrimages and retreats is somewhat blurred. The term pilgrim comes from the Latin *peregrinus*, which means 'stranger' and therefore one who has travelled; while retreat is from the Latin *retrahere*, meaning to 'draw back'. This suggests that the former is more associated with movement and the latter with stillness, but in both cases the attitude of mind should be the same, a watching and an openness to direct experience, without presuppositions or specific expectations. Like pilgrimages, retreats can be undertaken at any time and in any place. It is no more essential to withdraw from the City in order to go on retreat than it is when going on a pilgrimage.

Both pilgrimages and retreats can be solitary or taken in the company of others, though the latter, which typically involves at least some individual meditation, usually includes periods of silence. Meditation was discussed in Chapter 6, so all I want to touch on now is the importance of silence. Why silence? I said in Chapter 1 that the City is a metaphor not only for the outer world but also for our conscious minds. These minds are continually tuned into and invaded by the noise and clamour of the City, so that the confusion all around us is mirrored by the confusion going on in our own minds. When things fall silent, there is no longer anything to be confused. And just as a pilgrimage or a retreat takes us to a place in the outer world where the noise of the City is stilled, so it takes us to an inner place where the noise of our thinking also subsides.

I have a friend who treats the first half hour of the working day as his opportunity for retreat. He gets to work early (which also helps him to miss the worst of the traffic and thus to arrive in a relaxed frame of mind), and before his colleagues appear he sits in the quietness of his room preparing his mind for the hectic day that always lies ahead, absorbing something of the peace generated by the still space around him. By contrasting this stillness with the frantic activity that he knows will shortly fill the very same space for the next eight hours or so, his mind achieves a special kind of harmony. It is as if he moves outside himself, and sees that what happens in his own mind and what happens each day in his working environment are one and the same thing. Both are a succession of transitory, ever-changing events; and when the working day ends, both the room and his own mind will return to the stillness they are experiencing now.

There are moments during these small daily retreats when my friend experiences a complete harmony between his inner and outer worlds. He sits at his desk, allowing his

eyes to take in, without thought or judgement, th
he keeps on the wall, the photographs of family ar
and distant places on his desk, the plants at his window
(for like most people on a spiritual path he has a gift for
beautifying his environment), and as he does so the sense
of a person observing and of objects being observed disappears, and there is only an expansive feeling of being. Far
from rendering my friend unworldly, these quiet moments
at the start of the working day help make him particularly
effective at his job. He is a marvellous example of the
ability to cast out ambition, but to work as if one had
ambition (an important and profound spiritual teaching –
see Chapter 12). More relaxed, more objective, more clear-
sighted and more energetic than his colleagues, he has risen
seemingly effortlessly in his profession, liked and respected
by all who know him.

One of the values of opening the mind at the start of the
working day is that one frees it to do the job that lies ahead.
Much of our inefficiency is due to the fact that when
engaged on a task our minds are frequently elsewhere. We
are thinking about life outside work, or looking ahead to
the next job, or resenting the task itself, or feeling hostile
towards colleagues, or passing judgements, or longing for
the next tea-break, or engaged in any of 101 mental
activities unconnected with what we are actually supposed
to be doing. All this is not only extremely inefficient, it is
also very tiring. The mind wears itself out with its restless
activity, and with all the many mental conflicts it sets up in
the process.

Besides giving us the space to enjoy moments of quiet
revelation, a retreat therefore provides marvellous food for
the mind. The mind is not like a muscle, which gets
stronger simply through the act of use. It is much more
subtle than a physical organ, and the use which benefits it
has to be use of a very particular kind. A racing confusion
of thoughts and emotions exhausts rather than strengthens
it. The mind thrives upon stillness, and upon focused

thinking, upon an ordered harmony of movement that flows in one direction rather than being diverted this way and that by each distracting experience. Stillness and ordered movement strengthen and train the mind. Confusions, conflicts and inner clamour not only drain it of energy but retard its development, and can lead eventually to its breakdown.

This brings us back to the subject of a retreat. You can of course go on a retreat organized by a Buddhist, Christian or other religious group, and the City dweller should indeed make space to experience the tranquil atmosphere of these organized retreats from time to time if possible. But I am not concerned with them at present because, if you choose your organized retreats wisely, you will have a teacher or teachers who will give you all the guidance you need. My concern is with building retreat experiences into the busy life of the City. You may be unable or unwilling to emulate my friend and use the time at the beginning of the working day. But if so it is important to find an alternative space – weekly if not daily – to experience a short period of silence. The silence allows you just to be. And being is a central part of any retreat experience. Like my friend sitting at his desk, just being allows you to take in the mysterious business of your own existence. Do not attempt to follow any specific meditation practice at this time (meditation is an allied but nevertheless different exercise), but do not allow yourself to become distracted by anything (thoughts, other people, noise, obligations) that pulls you away from the direct experience of being who you are.

Just sit and take in what happens, without becoming stuck on any one thing. This is in fact a particularly receptive, tranquil form of the mindfulness described in Chapter 7. Keep the eyes, ears and mind open and allow them to register the moment-by-moment experience of being alive. The clock is ticking, a bird calls from the garden, the chair under you feels hard, there are many colours in the room, a memory of last summer surfaces, your breathing has a quiet, gentle rhythm, the door of the room is open, there is an awareness of yourself as a physical presence filling space, the landscape in the picture above the fireplace looks suddenly three-demensional, time is passing yet seems to stand still, a cloud covers the patch of blue sky seen through the window, there is a murmur of distant traffic, you have never noticed the pattern in the curtain before, a sudden breeze stirs the branches of the willow tree, how graceful the flowers are in the glass vase, and so on. Each experience is registered and then put down again, much as the breeze lifts and lets drop the willow branches.

At no point are you lost in thought. You are simply in each moment as it arises. For five minutes, ten minutes, however long you can spare, you are sitting in your room or in your garden or on a park bench 'retreating' from the usual ways of the world in order to experience that essence inside yourself from which your existence actually springs. If I can use the metaphor of a river for a moment, much of our life is spent downstream, where the water is churned up by every passing boat and clouded by pollution and the detritus of the City. And in this downstream world, we give no thought to where the river has its birth, to its life force in the clear springs of the tall mountains. We make the mistake of supposing that downstream is all there is, all we are, instead of tracing the river back to the purity of its source, and listening to its music. In these moments of retreat we are going upstream, beginning to find our way back, beginning to explore the unclouded experience of just being alive.

Do not expect anything mystical to happen. As with a pilgrimage, expectation gets in the way of direct experience. Just be there, in those quiet moments, noting without judging. After some experience of this exercise, you may well become aware of subtle changes in the way in which you view the world and yourself even when you are not in your moments of retreat. You may also be aware of greater equanimity and tranquillity in yourself, and an increase in the joy and freshness with which you go through the day. There may even be moments during the retreat itself which you describe afterwards as mystical, but expect and look for nothing. Just see what comes and how it comes.

Women, who are often innately better than men at this retreat exercise owing to their more sensitive, feeling-orientated approach to life, are paradoxically usually the first to protest that they do not have the time to stop and just *be* in this way. There are too many things to be done, too many jobs waiting. And when all the jobs are done they are just too tired. I have already made the point that an exercise of this kind releases some of the energy usually tied up in inner confusions, so that more gets accomplished during the day rather than less. The available time seems to expand rather than to contract, and one's ability to cope with stress seems to increase. In any case, what is our life about if we are unable to spare a few minutes a day or a week to experience it fully? Remember that the lotus only blooms in still waters.

Retaining Insights

I mentioned earlier that there is often a problem in retaining the insights or the state of mind that we experience in moments of pilgrimage and retreat. Not only does the busy life of the City seem to swamp them once we leave the stillness of the quiet room where they arose, but we find that even when we return to the stillness, they do not reappear. The same can be true of the profound states sometimes reached in meditation. There are several things we must do in order to handle this problem. The first two have already been mentioned, but they are worth re-emphasizing.

- Remember that this is the way our minds work. The mind is a constant process of change and flow, rather than a static receptacle into which we can put things and take them out again unchanged when we want them later. Never doubt the validity of the original experience simply because you cannot retain it in its original form.

- Do not allow expectation to come in the way of experience. We may have a wonderfully tranquil moment under our tree one summer evening, and then fall into the trap of expecting the moment to repeat itself in just that form the following day. The very act of expectation closes our mind, and thus prevents us from achieving the state in which this or any other profound experience can arise.

- Remember that each moment is a gift of grace. The original experience may never repeat itself, just as the birth of a child will never repeat itself. No matter. We had the experience and it was real enough, and even though we cannot re-create it, it will continue to feed us, just as our child continues to nurture us across the years.

- Do not discontinue the retreat experience and doubt its value just because it does not bring those special moments each time. As with meditation, much of value happens below the surface of our awareness. And in all work of this kind, perseverance and patience are vital. Benefits may seem long in coming, but each time we retreat into that quiet space we are laying their foundations.

CHAPTER 11

The Dreaming Mind

The Nature of Dreams

IN DREAMING, we retreat each night from the noise and confusion of the City and of normal consciousness. Dreams (and the evidence from sleep laboratories suggests that we all dream every night, whether we remember our dreams or not) are an entry into an altered state of consciousness that can provide insights not only into the hidden areas of our psychological life but into the even deeper levels of our spiritual self. None of the great psychospiritual traditions of the world has ignored the importance of dreams. The degree of emphasis has sometimes differed, but none of them has failed to recognize that dreams give access to areas of the mind denied to waking consciousness. It is only the scientific rationalism of the Western world – first in the 18th century and more especially in recent decades – that has attempted to relegate dreaming to the level of a kind of psychological dustbin, a jumbled downloading of unwanted fragments of memory and experience.

Anyone who takes the trouble to explore their dream world will quickly recognize the inadequacy of this rationalistic view. Dreaming is an essential activity of the mind, and dream content carries meaning which, once identified, can be put to use in the service of psychotherapy, personal growth and, above all, self-understanding. Ignoring our dreams is like ignoring those very places where we are likely to find important clues to the whereabouts of the lotus. To ignore dreams is to ignore vast areas of our own mind, and to remain strangers to a vital part of ourselves.

Think of dreams as representing the City by night. Familiar landmarks have faded into the darkness while others, unnoticeable by day, now come into view. The City by day has to do with rationality, with earning a living, and with our public and social roles. The City by night has to do with imagination, mysticism and the hidden face of the unconscious. The City by day is more concerned with materiality and logic, the City by night with intuition and the unseen.

To learn from dreams, we must first train ourselves to remember them. Fortunately, various methods of helping us are at hand (see, for example, Fontana 1994b and 1995 for more detail). The most important of them can be summarized as follows:

- Recognize the importance of dreams. If the conscious mind thinks dreams are unimportant, it will naturally try to discard them on waking. By acknowledging their value, this process is reversed.

- Tell yourself frequently during the day that you will remember your dreams. These reminders reprogramme the conscious mind to keep its attention turned inwards as it awakens. They should be repeated as you drift into sleep each night.

- If no dreams are recalled upon waking, focus upon any thoughts or feelings that happen to be present. These thoughts and feelings may have arisen from dreams, and may help to spark off dream memories. Research shows that we each dream for around two hours every night. There is plenty there to be remembered.

- Don't struggle for recall. Dreams emerge best i   ill calm mind. Do not try and recall them with the effort you often put into the recall of waking

The harder you try to do so, the more they are likely to elude you.

- Accept and value those fragments of dreams that you do manage to remember. Acknowledge them as carrying meaning, even if that meaning escapes you. Neglecting the small and apparently unimportant dreams discourages recall of dreams from a deeper level.

- Keep a notebook (a dream diary) by your bed, and write down your dream memories as soon as you can after waking. No matter how firmly they seem to be lodged in your memory, dreams usually fade quickly.

- Get into the habit of thinking back to your dreams during the day. Reread your notes. Regard your dream life as a kind of parallel existence that can be recalled and reviewed in similar detail to your waking life. In past centuries the Chinese believed that consciousness leaves the body in dreams and travels in other worlds, while the Greeks thought that dreams are messages from the gods. Read about these and other cultural notions and ponder how dream content could have given rise to them.

- Be patient. It may take days or even months before you are regularly remembering dreams, but success comes with perseverance. When working intensively on my dreams, I recall on average five or six each morning, and there is nothing remarkable about this. You can speed things up by occasionally setting an alarm clock to wake you during the night. We usually dream in four or five episodes during the hours of sleep, and the alarm may wake you during one of them. If you are too drowsy to make notes when roused, speak your dream memories into a tape recorder. Note how, when you listen to them the following day, they may already have vanished from conscious memory.

Dream Interpretation

Dreams are almost always presented in a symbolic language which must be understood if we are to interpret them correctly. Dreams are the language of the unconscious, which seems to prefer visual images to words. All the great spiritual traditions teach that the mind must sometimes turn away from words if it is to experience itself. Words, for all their power, beauty and usefulness, dominate our mental processes, and we need experiences beyond words if these processes are to reveal themselves in their naked essence. Words prompt us to talk *about*, and have ideas *about*, reality, rather than to experience it directly. Dreams are not bound by words, and their meaning is not bound by the logical thinking created by words.

Some of the symbols used in dreams are personal to the dreamer. We each build up an array of associations over the years which carry meaning for us but for nobody else. For example, a child who curls up in a favourite chair when reading story books may come to associate the colour and pattern of the chair with the stories. Another child may associate a particular song with the mother who sings it each night at bedtime. Thus the colour and pattern of the chair and the music of the song serve as highly personal symbols of the pleasures of reading, and of the presence of a loving mother. In later life, both symbols will be capable of evoking powerful early memories in the individuals concerned.

However, other symbols carry a more universal meaning, as evidenced by their appearance across diverse cultures and centuries. Their appeal appears to be innate, and to have little to do with individual learning. To all intents and purposes they have emerged ready-made from what Jung called the collective unconscious (Chapter 4), and carry a compelling, evocative power for all who work with them. One group of examples consists of geometrical shapes such as the cross, the circle, the triangle, the square and the star, all of which feature prominently in the rituals and sacred art of the world's great religions. Others are associated with archetypal characters and events of the great myths and legends of the world (also discussed in Chapter 4).

In interpreting dreams, we have to learn to identify both personal symbols and universal symbols, and then tease out their meaning. The former symbols are more likely to feature in what Jung called small dreams, dreams which carry only average emotional force and which are likely to be quickly forgotten unless they are recorded, and the latter in what he called grand dreams, those dreams which have a powerful numinous quality and which can remain fresh in the mind many years afterwards. But for both small and grand dreams, the method of interpretation is the same.

1 List the separate aspects of the dream under such headings as *scenery and objects*, *characters*, *events*, *colours* and *emotions*. Do not strive for detailed accuracy. The categories may overlap and the memories associated with them may be confused. But do not ignore apparently unimportant details. These can carry the deepest meaning.

2 Select one of the categories and subject the items it contains to *direct association*. This technique, developed by Jung, involves writing each item in the centre of a sheet of paper, and writing around it all the associations it evokes. After each association return to the original item; do not allow each association to spark off associations of its own (as is done in the Freudian technique of *free association*). Keep the associations as specific as possible – for example, if the dream was of a red car, the associations must be to a red car and not to a car of any other colour.

Jung observed that the process of association is assisted if the dreamer imagines he or she is describing the dream

item to someone for whom it is unfamiliar. Thus the
associations to 'dog' might be animal, domestic pet, four
legs, barks, hunts, faithful friend, runs fast, chases cats,
bites, carnivorous, nice to stroke, can frighten children,
fights other dogs, and so on. Each of the associations
concerned is something symbolized by the dog, and any
one (or more) of them could help reveal the message that it
is intended symbolically to convey.

Having done this, decide which of these associations is
more likely to be the correct one. Jung suggested that the
decision is helped if the dreamer looks for *elaborations* in
response to any of the individual associations – if there are
particularly strong personal reactions or responses to any
of them. For example the dreamer might remember being
chased and terrified by a dog as a child, or watching a
sheepdog at work during an idyllic summer holiday.
Sometimes elaborations arouse intense emotions, or
involve the retrieval of memories that have long been
forgotten by the conscious mind.

If the process of elaboration suggests that all the
associations concerned are of a personal nature, the dream
probably arises from your personal unconscious, but if it
appears to contain universal archetypal material it may be
from the collective unconscious. If this appears to be the
case, a process called *amplification* may be needed to
identify its meaning. Amplification involves seeking parallels between the dream and the vast storehouse of
archetypal myths, legends and fairy tales in world literature (Chapter 4). As this storehouse and your dream
both have their source in the collective unconscious, it is
unimportant whether you knew of such myths and legends
before the dream occurred or not. The myth-making quality
of the collective unconscious can generate the profound
themes involved even if they have never previously been a
part of your conscious thinking.

Amplification should not be embarked upon for dreams
that do not contain archetypal material, as it can obscure

more personal meanings. But where a genuine parallel is identified between the dream and a particular myth, the latter can be studied in order to see what parallels it suggests with your own life, and therefore what guidance or warnings it seems to provide. This presupposes a readiness to study the enduring myths, legends and stories of the world, but these are in any case a treasure trove for all those on a spiritual path, representing as they do profound symbolic truths about the deepest levels of our psychological and spiritual realities.

For the Westerner, Babylonian, Egyptian and Greek myths are likely to reveal their symbolic meaning most readily, but the native American, Indian and Chinese myths carry similar psychological and spiritual force when properly understood. The classic works of Sir James Frazer, Joseph Campbell and Carl Jung (listed in the Bibliography) provide invaluable introductions to the mythological world, and Campbell and Jung also provide guidance on the links between myths and dreams. A knowledge of the great myths of the world and of universal symbols such as those I have described elsewhere (Fontana 1994b) is the best way to learn how to amplify and understand those dreams which go beyond the personal unconscious and dip into the bottomless depths of the collective mind.

Self-Insights from Dreaming

The meaning of a dream has been uncovered when we are sure it provides self-insights that ring true. Some of these insights may be indications of psychological and spiritual progress and/or of the difficulties and decisions that face us on the path. Amplification of a grand dream in the light of mythological material may leave you identified for example with the symbolic challenges and temptations met with by Jason and the Argonauts in their search for the golden fleece, or by Hercules in his descent into the labyrinth, or by Ishtar in her journey through the underworld to meet her dark sister Ereshkigal. But we must be sure that these insights really do ring true, and not grasp them just because they seem attractive. To this end, Jung suggests that we should apply three tests to any dream interpretation.

- Does it 'act' for you – ie does it 'set your life in motion again' by giving you some indication of the way ahead, or some new courage and inspiration?

- Is the interpretation confirmed (or contradicted) by subsequent dreams? A dream diary allows you to recognize recurring dreams, as well as recurring themes within dreams, and dreams which form a sequence of some kind. Do these support your original interpretation?

- Is the interpretation confirmed (or contradicted) by events in waking life? As the barriers between waking consciousness and dream consciousness begin to dissolve, you will see more clearly how the guidance given in dreams fits in with daily life. If a dream appears to give a false message, do not blame the dream, blame your interpretation of it.

Above all, Jung stressed that no dream interpretation should be forced upon the dreamer by a psychotherapist or anyone else – it must always ring true for the dreamer. A psychotherapist or psychologist well versed in dream theory and experienced at helping clients work with their dreams can facilitate interpretation, and make suggestions and give advice, but he or she should never attempt to impose an interpretation upon you.

Lucid Dreaming

From ancient times, both Eastern sages and Western followers of the esoteric tradition have taught that psycho-

‚al and spiritual development depends in large measure upon harmony and communication between conscious
and unconscious levels of the mind. Ultimately, the barriers
between conscious and unconscious disappear altogether,
and the whole of the inner life becomes accessible to
consciousness (it is said that the Buddha was even able to
remember each of his many thousands of previous lives).

One result of this is that consciousness is able to run
continuously throughout waking, dreaming and dreamless
sleep. Consciousness in dreamless sleep is akin to a state of
deep meditation, free of thoughts and images and charged
with acute, unwavering, profound awareness. Only very
advanced practitioners are able to achieve this state.
Consciousness in dreaming is much more common however, and is associated with the phenomenon known as *lucid
dreaming*. In a lucid dream, the dreamer is fully conscious
that he or she is dreaming, and experiences dream events
with an awareness similar to that in waking life. In
addition, lucid dreams are free from much of the irration-
ality and discontinuity that characterize normal dreaming,
and during them the dreamer may have access to all the
memories and thought functions of waking life.

Usually the awareness of a lucid dream dawns abruptly.
The dreamer is in the middle of a conventional dream
when something – perhaps an illogicality or an inaccuracy
in dream scenery or events – alerts the mind to the fact that
this must be a dream. The experience is quite unmistakable,
and often accompanied by a surge of excitement and what
can best be described as a feeling of mind expansion.
Colours stand out with a particular brightness, as if a veil
has been stripped away, and objects take on an illuminated
clarity that can even surpass waking experience. Perhaps
the most remarkable aspect of lucid dreaming is that the
dreamer becomes able to control the dream, to decide
where to go and what to do, even to experiment with the
dream environment. Yet the lucid dream never loses its
seemingly objective reality. The decision to visit a tropical

Myths and Dreams

As we saw in Chapter 4, the enduring fascination of the great myths and legends of the world lies in the fact that they both arise from, and speak directly to, the human psyche. They are symbolic representations of the primal hopes, dreams and fears of each one of us, route maps of our journey towards wholeness and happiness that mark out the challenges, temptations, assistance and pitfalls faced by us on the way. There is thus a sense in which whether they are historically true or not is unimportant. The fact that they have survived down the centuries indicates that they say something truthful about the human condition. They are in a sense a prescientific body of psychological knowledge, more accurate and more helpful in many ways than many of our modern psychological theories.

Grand dreams arise from the same level of the human mind as these myths and legends, and thus the content of the former can in many ways mimic that of the latter, or possess close associations with it. It is for this reason that myths are so valuable in dream amplification. The dreamer sees the association between his or her dream and the myth, recognizes that the myth is appropriate to his or her circum-stances, and then studies it to see if it has anything to teach about present or future behaviour.

For example, a member of a dream workshop had a recurring dream of swimming across a dark and troubled stretch of water guided by something or someone on the opposite shore. When he reached the shore, he was aware of receiving a joyous greeting, and of a golden light which turned night into day. Yet the dream often left him feeling incomplete and troubled. In the course of dream amplification, he saw an association with the myth of Leander, who swims each night across the Hellespont guided by a light placed there by his mistress, Hero. One night there is a great storm, Hero's light is extinguished, and losing his way in the blackness Leander is swept out to sea and drowned. In dreams the sea often symbolizes the unconscious, and the dreamer identified Hero with the archetype of the mysterious young woman who symbolizes innate wisdom, and who appears frequently in myths to provide guidance through a hostile landscape or seascape. However, the dream seemed to be saying that, essential as our intuition is as a guide on the spiritual path, we should not rely upon it alone. Its light may fail us when we meet extreme challenges in the inner life.

At the time the dreamer was stubbornly independent in his spiritual practice, going on long solitary meditation retreats and being very dismissive of the need for a teacher. He took the dream as a warning that if he continued in this way he would before long be overwhelmed by the material being released from his unconscious, and that he should begin the search for a reliable outer teacher without delay.

island may be the dreamer's own, but on arrival the island will be just as novel as an island seen for the first time in waking life.

Israel Regardie, a leading expert on the Western mystery traditions, writes (Regardie 1972) that the advanced adept experiences all his or her dreams in this lucid state, and thus

'no longer passes the night in deep oblivion or at best in the phantastic adventure of [non-lucid] dream...[but]...with the consciousness retained during sleep. There is no long gap of oblivion: all is one continuous, free-flowing stream of awareness.

Developing Lucid Dreaming

As our personal and spiritual development increases (and in particular as our powers of meditation and mindfulness improve), lucid dreams tend to become increasingly common. But there are a number of practices that can help us develop lucid dreaming, and these are summarized below (the interested reader might also like to see the guidance given in my two books on dreaming listed in the Bibliography).

- Tell yourself frequently during the day, and in particular just before going to sleep, that when you enter the dream world, you will be aware that you are dreaming. The unconscious is very open to being reprogrammed (this is largely what happens in hypnosis), and the secret here is to give it frequent instructions, keeping them short, and very specific. Do not lose patience if results are slow in coming. Your failure to take your dreams seriously has meant that you have been programming the unconscious to ignore them for most of your life so far. This takes time to rectify.

- Ask yourself frequently during the day 'How do I know that I am not dreaming now?' Notice all those things by which you habitually recognize that you are awake (eg things behaving lawfully and pre-dictably, the ability to read, familiar objects remaining in their rightful places). As you become more and more aware of the differences between the waking world and the dream world, so you will become better able to spot the anomalies in the latter that will remind you that you are dreaming.

- Keep reminding yourself during the day that you will see a particular object in your dreams, prefera-bly a familiar object that is likely to crop up regularly. When you see this object, it will remind you that you are dreaming. Castaneda (most recently 1993) was advised by his teacher to concentrate on seeing his hands. Even so, it took him two years before this led him into lucid dreaming.

- Imagine you are dreaming while still awake. See everything as an illusion created by your mind, which you can change at will. The same feeling of being in charge of your own reality will then, with practice, be carried over into dreaming.

Two other methods involve first going through each dream memory and asking yourself why this or that event did not prompt you into knowing you were dreaming, and secondly putting an object in a special place each night and telling yourself that you will visit it in your dream body, and become aware you are dreaming the moment you succeed.

Like other authorities, Regardie sees lucid dreaming as both an aid towards, and a sign of, psychospiritual progress, and modern research seems to bear this out in that habitual lucid dreamers appear less prone to depression and neuroses than most people (see Garfield 1991). They are also more aware of the infinite potential of their own minds.

In addition, by taking control of their dreaming, lucid dreamers are able to tune in much more effectively to the wisdom of the unconscious. During a lucid dream we can tell ourselves to visit a spiritual teacher, and find ourselves face to face with an archetypal figure such as the wise old man or woman, or Isis or another goddess of mysteries, or an animal with human speech, or one of the gods. The wisdom may be conveyed to us in words, or in the form of a symbol or talisman of some kind. It is unnecessary to speculate on whether these dream teachers have objective reality or whether they are creations of our own minds (or a combination of the two). The important thing is that the teachings we receive from them may be invaluable in our search for the lotus.

In Eastern traditions it is believed that the lucid dreamer can also visit – or be visited by – his or her living teacher during dreams, and when I am asked if I think such a belief is true or not, my reply is that only when one has developed lucid dreaming and put it to the test will one be able to know for sure one way or the other. The same applies to the Western esoteric belief that lucid dreamers can meet each other in dreams and actually share the dream content (Richardson, 1985, gives accounts of experiences of this kind).

The Nyingma school of Tibetan Buddhism (the oldest of the schools) teaches in addition that lucid dreaming – and the maintenance of consciousness through dreamless sleep – is invaluable to those on the spiritual path because sleep and dreaming are a nightly dress rehearsal for death. By remaining conscious throughout sleep and dreaming, we learn how to remain conscious throughout the act of dying, and thus remain in control of what happens to us in the after-death state. Such teachings may seem strange to the Western mind. All I can say is that I have received them from teachers who struck me as knowing exactly what they were talking about.

CHAPTER 12

Living in the City: The Practical Issues

FOLLOWING A SPIRITUAL PATH involves paying attention to the way in which we live both our inner and our outer lives, and both of these areas are addressed throughout this book. However, we must keep in mind that any sharp distinction between the two worlds is unreal, because what we do in one intimately informs and affects what we do in the other. Nowhere is this more obvious than when we address two major problems of the spiritual life, namely how we find time in the busy outer world to turn the mind inwards, and how we decide on the code of moral conduct that should govern our dealings with everything else that shares with us the miraculous gift of existence.

Finding the Time

This is less of a problem than might at first appear. People are forever saying to me that they would like to meditate or read improving books or attend classes or go on retreats (or even become writers or artists) if only they could find the time. The short answer is that we find time for the things we really want to do. The sad fact is that much of our time is in fact wasted. We fritter it away as if it were renewable income rather than steadily diminishing capital. No matter how busy we claim to be, if we really want the time to

follow spiritual practices then we do not have to 'find' it –
it is there already. All we have to do is to make the
commitment to use it.

But there is a longer answer. A large part of the spiritual
life has to do with using the mind, and in fact we are using
the mind continually anyway. We are using it in order to
become lost in thought, to distract ourselves by mental
chatter, to daydream, to think of the future or dwell on the
past, and to rehearse the answers we should have given to
the last person with whom we exchanged angry words. As
we saw when discussing meditation and mindfulness in
Chapters 6 and 7, it is possible to train the mind to stay
much more focused and concentrated than this, and thus
enable ourselves to make much better use of our mental
space. Spirituality is not just about turning our attention to
spiritual thoughts, it is about bringing a new level of
mental awareness into all we do, so that we become more
in tune with moment-by-moment experience, and with the
real meaning of what it is to be alive.

This allows us to be far more aware, not only of ourselves
as a conscious spark of existence moving through time and
space, but of other people – their motives, difficulties,
strengths and vulnerabilities – and of the physical world,
with its beauty, its life and its abundance of phenomena. In
a very real sense, our outer behaviour thus becomes a
reflection of our inner life, while the inner life is constantly
being renewed and enriched by our outer experience.

By virtue of this more effective use of our own minds,
part of the problem of 'finding' time for spiritual practice is
solved. Life itself becomes a spiritual practice, in the best
and most vigorous and useful sense of the term. There will,
however, be occasions when we want to focus the mind
specifically upon spiritual issues and experiences, and
these are largely dealt with in the discussions of pilgrimages and retreats in Chapter 10 and of meditation in
Chapter 6. The only thing to add is that we should as far as
possible identify a set time each day when we can focus

specifically upon a chosen spiritual practice.

This requires a certain amount of the self-discipline, patience and perseverance essential to spiritual progress (just as they are essential to progress in any worthwhile undertaking). The set time may be first thing in the morning or last thing at night, during our lunch-break, when we arrive at the office or when we arrive home in the evening, or any other time. Initially it may only be five minutes, or the time it takes us to walk through a favourite park at lunchtime, but usually we find the time extending automatically as our practice deepens. But setting aside the same time (or times) each day trains the mind to turn automatically towards the spiritual practice concerned when the time approaches. For a practice such as meditation, sitting always in the same place serves to turn the mind in the appropriate direction, although when meditation is well established it can also be done anywhere we choose – sitting on the bus, waiting for the train, relaxing for a few minutes before going into a meeting or between the completion of one task and the commencement of the next.

A Code of Moral Conduct

The second problem, deciding on a code of moral conduct that can inform our lives in the City, requires more discussion. If we turn to the great spiritual traditions for help, we find that they all teach such a code in some detail, and stress its importance not only as a facilitator of social living but as an essential if individuals are to attain spiritual enlightenment or salvation. To many Westerners, the Ten Commandments, revealed through Moses on Mount Sinai, is the best-known of these codes, while some of the most extensive are those followed in Buddhist monasteries, which can number over 300 items (most of them designed essentially to keep the monk acutely aware

The Use of Time

Many people tell me they feel guilty if they give time to themselves. Their minds are always upon other things they 'ought' to be doing. But giving time to oneself is essential for both psychological and spiritual development. When I explore these feelings of guilt with the people concerned, we often find that many date back to early conditioning. During childhood, they were made to feel idle and valueless unless they were doing something 'useful'. The worst thing of all was to be caught doing nothing.

Maslow, whose work is looked at in connection with the mature personality in Chapter 9, once lamented that there are no chapters in psychology textbooks on 'loafing about'. He was right. There should be such chapters, because 'loafing about' is often a synonym for giving time to ourselves. Provided the mind is not being pulled this way and that by mental chatter, it can often be a wonderful way of *being* as opposed to constantly *doing*.

A very great deal of useless 'doing' goes on in the world. At a conservative estimate, 70 per cent of the people in a developed country earn their living doing things that are of no real value to anyone. And 70 per cent of people spend their leisure hours doing things (like sitting slumped in front of the television set watching mindless rubbish) that are of no real value either. Thus finding time for oneself in the course of which the sense of being becomes far more important than the sense of doing is of immeasurably more value than at least 70 per cent of the things with which we so busily occupy our time.

Keeping physically fit, going to yoga or tai chi classes, practising deep relaxation (which cannot be done while attempting to do anything else at the same

time), playing music, painting, walking in the countryside, reading things that inspire or enlighten,
meditation, all involve giving time to ourselves, and all
– provided we are doing them for the moment-by-
moment experience instead of for some extrinsic goal
– allow us to put being before doing.

This does not mean that all 'own time' activities are
equally worthwhile from the standpoint of inner
development. The nature of the experience must also
come into the equation. Yoga and meditation are
obviously of more value in a developmental sense
than playing patience or hunting the thimble. But
anything that allows the mind to stay fully absorbed
in what it is doing can lead to what is sometimes called
a 'Zen state', that is a state in which any sense of
separation between the self and the task disappears,
and the normal everyday consciousness is replaced
by a timeless moment of pure delight.

of what he or she is doing in each waking moment).

The great majority of these moral codes were formulated
centuries ago, and in the context of societies and cultures
very different from those existing today. So what relevance,
if any, do they have for modern life in the City? And to
what extent have they been superseded by our own civil
and criminal laws?

In spite of certain differences, most of the codes contain
strictures against killing sentient beings, theft, falsehood,
sexual misconduct, alcohol and other intoxicants. These are
for the most part also enshrined in the various civil laws of
the land, and help us live together in peace and harmony.
But they have a deeper purpose, helping the individual to
achieve a self-transformation that will ultimately bring him
or her closer to the divine. They enable the individual to
gain the 'merit' that will help him or her after death either

to gain entry into the heavenly realms, or to obtain a more propitious rebirth next time around. As such, they are seen as an essential backdrop to the inner spiritual practices of meditation and prayer. One cannot, so the teachings go, follow these inner practices effectively unless one works simultaneously to purify one's behaviour in the outer world.

Why is this? To explore matters further, we can look in turn at each of these strictures, and also examine their relevance to modern living.

Killing Sentient Beings

The term 'sentient beings' includes all those living organisms which appear capable of experiencing feelings, from humans on the one hand down to the smallest insects on the other. Doubtless when this prohibition against killing was first formulated it was thought that all sentient beings were visible to the naked eye, and that with reasonable care one could avoid doing them harm. We now know, of course, that the microscopic world contains many more inhabitants than the macroscopic world. Each time we splash germicide down the kitchen sink or take an antibiotic against infection, we slaughter bacteria by the millions. Each time the farmer sprays his crops, each time hospital staff incinerate infected dressings, the death-toll mounts ever higher. And at each moment of every day, unremarked by our conscious minds, our own immune systems are fighting off invading armies of potentially lethal micro-organisms.

In view of this wholesale slaughter, is it any longer important – or even practical – to try to avoid taking life, other than human life? If moral codes are designed to help our own development as well as to protect others, the answer must be 'yes'. We have no way of knowing whether humble organisms like wasps or beetles feel pain when we put our foot upon them, but a moment's self-observation reveals the brutalizing effect such an action has upon *us*. We have extinguished a life, thoughtlessly and usually entirely unnecessarily. Is this all the reverence we have for life, in spite of the fact that the same life force animates the creature we have just destroyed as animates ourselves?

By contrast, sweeping up the insect concerned and putting it outside gives us a precious moment of caring for something much smaller and weaker than ourselves. Such an act helps to refine our reverence for life, and helps sensitize us to the value and meaning of existence. We cannot always be as stoical as the Buddhist monks of Sri Lanka and South-East Asia, who will sit calmly in meditation while mosquitoes descend upon them in clouds, but the practice of refraining from unnecessarily killing any sentient creature must be integral to any spiritual training. Sogyal Rinpoche, one of the Tibetan teachers who has helped bring Buddhist teachings to the West, sums this up when he says that we should practise *ahimsa*, non-violence, towards all life *'so far as is possible'*.

The profundity of this teaching lies in the responsibility it lays upon us to ponder what is meant in each situation by 'so far as is possible'. Is it possible to put the unwanted insect outside alive rather than dead? Is it possible to be well-nourished without the ill-treatment and slaughter each day of thousands of farm animals? Is it possible to achieve pest control by any means other than wholesale spraying with toxic chemicals? Is it possible (at the highest level of all) to operate a system of justice without the judicial murder of wrongdoers, and to settle disputes between countries and communities without resorting to the bomb and the bullet?

The answer in each case seems obvious enough, as are the consequences for our own inner development.

Theft

Theft is usually interpreted as taking anything not freely given, a notion that raises no end of problems in the modern world. First, there is the question of the importance of whatever is taken. It is sometimes claimed that taking a paper clip without the permission of our employer is as bad as rifling the till, but the criminal law clearly takes a different view. The first offence would be regarded as too trivial to notice, the second would merit a gaol sentence.

Secondly, there is the problem of what is meant by 'taking anything not freely given'. Currency speculators can 'take' billions of pounds from a country's financial reserves simply by buying and selling at the touch of a computer button. This money is hardly 'taken' with the consent of the people who have originally earned it, and whose jobs may now be destroyed because of it. Politicians can vote themselves vast salary increases, and travel the world on unnecessary missions financed by taxpayers, the majority of whom would certainly not regard their money as 'freely given' for such purposes.

Thirdly, there are the problems raised by poverty and underprivilege. If a poor man or woman steals from the rich in order to feed a starving family, this is certainly taking something that is not freely given; yet if the alternative is to allow children to die of starvation, can this really be classed as stealing?

A fourth problem has to do with the operation of the civil and criminal law itself. To fine a wrongdoer or to deprive him or her of liberty (or worse still of life) is certainly to take something that is not freely given. Yet without sanctions of some kind against wrongdoers, albeit as humane as possible, society would find it hard to exercise social control over all its members.

A fifth difficulty has to do with the theft of time: leaving work a few minutes early, working more slowly than we reasonably can, taking a longer lunch break, going sick when we want the odd day off, using the firm's time to do some of our private work, engaging in personal conversations in the firm's time, taking private telephone calls in working hours (to say nothing of making them), etc. All these involve taking something that is not freely given. Yet is it realistic to use every minute of the working day for the purpose for which it is intended, particularly if we feel our employers transgress in the first place by undervaluing us or paying poor wages?

These are a few of the obvious difficulties we face when deciding what is meant by taking things not freely given. But there are others that are less obvious. Is accepting money for expenses which we secretly know need not be incurred (or worse still will not be incurred) tantamount to taking things not freely given? Is failing to pay a bill or to return borrowed money until the last possible moment taking something not freely given? Is inflating an insurance claim, by however little? Is avoiding customs duties by failing to declare items on return from a holiday abroad, or employing a clever accountant to avoid legitimate tax liabilities, or accepting business perks in place of salary as a way of doing the same thing?

And there are difficulties on the other side of the coin as well. In some circumstances things may be freely given, yet we can question whether it is right freely to accept them. An obvious instance is gambling, which in many ways is as damaging to family life as the misuse of alcohol. Is accepting a gambler's money, knowing full well that the odds are heavily stacked against him or her getting it back, equivalent to stealing? Is taking money for the sale of harmful substances like tobacco? Is voting for a government that accepts money for the sale of weapons of war?

In a small rural or even urban society it may be simple enough to decide what is meant by taking things not freely given, but is such a thing possible in our complex modern world? Why not take the easy way out, and limit ourselves to staying on the right side of the civil and criminal law? In any case, most business enterprises accept that the pilfering of materials and time by employees is bound to take place, and simply pay everyone a little less to compensate for it, or marginally put up the price of their goods and services to the public.

Before agreeing, we should apply the same criterion as we did when discussing the killing of sentient beings, and ask what effect casual petty theft has upon us. However large and impersonal the organization from which the theft takes place, the consequence for ourselves is to coarsen our respect for our own integrity. We do not care enough about ourselves to bother whether we are honest or dishonest. In addition, taking things which are not earned or freely given lessens our respect for the things concerned. They do not come to us as a reward for our own labour or as a result of the good wishes of others, but as the outcome of an act of casual theft.

Each person must decide for him- or herself the resolution of the various difficulties (some of them highly complex) listed above. Too much rigid dogma risks getting in the way of personal responsibility. But the essential thing is to be aware of the effect our behaviour has not only upon others but upon ourselves. This can be brought home by reflecting on the way in which we seek to justify our actions when taking things not freely given: 'No-one will miss it'; 'I've earned it anyway'; 'It's compensation for the way I've been treated'; 'It would only be wasted if I don't take it'; 'Everybody does it'; 'The boss is as much on the fiddle as we are'. Such justifications demean our own levels of understanding. And once we de-sensitize ourselves in this way to the taking of small things, it becomes easier and easier to justify taking something bigger. In addition, we risk blurring the distinction between right and wrong, until in the end even our freedom to take correct decisions becomes impaired.

Among other things, this can lead to a fragmentation of our personality. A dichotomy develops between the 'moral' person who operates in our domestic and social lives, and the 'amoral' person who takes over in all other areas. Such fragmentation is directly harmful to psychological and spiritual growth, which lays emphasis upon wholeness and integration within all aspects of our being. (A similar fragmentation can result if we reverse things and make a great show of integrity in our public life, while ill-treating and exploiting those nearest to us.) Not for nothing does Buddhism stress that moral precepts are actually vows that we make to our own higher nature!

Falsehood

As with theft, the definition and practical meaning of falsehood or lying presents a number of difficulties. To tell a lie means to state that which, to the best of our knowledge and belief, is untrue. But are lies justified in order to protect the feelings and the vulnerabilities of others? And what of lies which, though not factually true, nevertheless contain 'poetic' truth in that they convey correct concepts and ideas? And what about metaphors and symbols, both in the things we tell our children (for example the existence of Father Christmas or the tooth fairy), and in the mythical elements contained in the great religions themselves? And what of the ways in which, to keep up our spirits or because we are incurably optimistic by nature, we sometimes knowingly mislead ourselves?

In addition, what about those situations when we say something that is perfectly true, but which is only part of the whole answer, or which we know will actually mislead others? And those occasions when, acting on the premise that ignorance is bliss, we turn a blind eye to some matter of which by rights we should take notice, or keep silent and allow others to go on believing something which we know to be untrue, and which is to their obvious disadvantage?

Similarly, what of those occasions when we lie to hide

our own feelings or to avoid self-disclosure: 'No of course I'm not frightened/angry/upset/excited' and so on? Clearly this is engaging just as much in falsehood as when we lie about external facts. Sometimes we do it in order to protect our own inner lives, sometimes to give a good impression of ourselves, and sometimes to deceive people into thinking that they do not have the power to engage us emotionally.

Conversely, what about the instances when the truth is used ostensibly to give information but in reality to cause harm and upset, as happens for example in the 'revelations' about the private lives of celebrities which are regularly featured in the tabloid press, or when we remind others of past mistakes for which they have already atoned? No overt lies are involved in either of these examples, yet there is clear dishonesty about the motivation involved.

The more we delve into the subject of truth and untruth, the more we realize what a tangled and difficult issue it is. And what, in any case, *is* truth? When Pilate put the question to him, Christ, on the only occasion recorded in the Gospels, refrained from answering. Is truth therefore relative? By lying on certain occasions, are we not more true to our underlying convictions, which may be to avoid giving information which we know will wound? The problem about lying, however, is that once we start the practice, it becomes difficult to know where to draw the line. Before we know it, the distinction between fact and fiction becomes blurred. Falsehood becomes the easy way out, and ultimately we fail to be true not only to others but to ourselves.

If people ask us for directions in the City, we try to be as accurate as possible in our reply. We have no wish to let them lose their way in the backstreets and alleyways. Yet to give any sort of information which we know to be factually inaccurate is to mislead in much the same way as sending someone in the wrong direction. We may assume that by giving false information we are protecting another person from suffering, but in fact we may be actively hindering their development. The usual example that people bring forward is when, out of politeness, we tell a friend we think what they are wearing looks nice, when in fact we are convinced it represents a woeful lack of taste. A more honest answer might have encouraged them to think again, and perhaps decide on something more suitable. Of course, there are kind and unkind ways of making our honest opinion known, but without this honest opinion, our friend is denied the chance to develop a better dress sense.

This trivial example can be stretched to cover all aspects of our relationships with other people. The truth may often hurt initially, but it may be of great help in the long run. In this context, awkward and difficult people, and those who perhaps dislike us, can sometimes be of more help to us than our best friends, as such people may not hesitate to tell us home truths about ourselves. Although their motives in so doing may be suspect, these truths can be of enormous value in helping us to take a longer look at ourselves. Where our friends hold back, our enemies are more forthright. The American spiritual teacher Ram Dass reminded me of this when he once remarked: 'Have you noticed that all your friends like you?' Certainly all our friends like us, and it is this liking that sometimes comes between them and a readiness to be more open with us.

Conversely, a similar lack of openness exists when we hide our feelings from others. The urge against self-disclosure is very strong in some of us, and few things are more inappropriate in human relationships than the compulsion to spill out all the messy details about ourselves to all and sundry. But an excessive aversion to self-disclosure means that we shut off a large part of ourselves from others. We pretend to be somebody we are not. This hinders intimacy, and distances other people from us and us from them. As we saw in Chapter 9, psychologically healthy people do not talk unnecessarily about themselves, but they answer direct questions openly and frankly. Talking compulsively about ourselves indicates a lack of inner strength and self-sufficiency; refusal to talk about ourselves indicates a lack of trust both in the validity of our own feelings and in the likely reaction of other people to them.

Colleagues and Power

Honesty towards colleagues and friends raises a number of related issues of great importance in the spiritual life. Should we always be honest when it comes to telling people our real feelings for them, particularly if these involve negative emotions or judgements? And if we are convinced that colleagues answerable to us are not suited to the posts they hold, should we say so and cause them to lose their jobs (even though we may know this will be very damaging for them)?

Some of the biggest issues that face us in the City are conflicts of roles and loyalties in the workplace. These go beyond issues just of honesty, and raise questions as to whether we should be *people-centred* (concerned primarily for the welfare of individuals) or *problem-centred* (concerned primarily with solving problems, even at the cost of hurting others). Or should we try to meet each situation on its merits, even if it means appearing to act inconsistently?

Spiritual teachings are strangely inconclusive on these matters. Christ made clear that we should render unto Caesar the things that are Caesar's, but he also prevented the woman taken in adultery from receiving the standard (and inhuman) punishment for her behaviour. This suggests that in such matters it is purposely left to us to be responsible for our own decisions. It is dogma that leads to the excesses of the Inquisition and of totalitarian political regimes.

Provided we are acting out of a genuine humanity and a proper understanding of the other person and the issues involved, then we must make our decision and take full responsibility for whatever consequences follow.

In other areas of human relationships in the workplace, the spiritual teachings are clear and unequivocal. The more we act out of ego, the less we act out of sensitivity and concern for others. Power in particular can be a big stumbling block to those on the spiritual path, because power flatters the ego, and deceives us into believing that we are better than our fellow men and women. But power applied wisely and fairly and with no thought of personal gain can be a great blessing to all. If you are in a position of power, it is well to keep four simple questions in the forefront of your mind.

- Why am I given this power?

- Who is benefitting from my exercise of it?

- Am I prepared to relinquish it the moment circumstances indicate it should pass to another?

- How will I feel about myself when I *have* relinquished it?

Little need be said about what the answers to such questions reveal.

In a highly complex area like truth and falsehood it may be impossible to lay down detailed absolutes. What is important, however, is that we work out a code of conduct, dictated by a genuine desire to use truth as a way of helping others (even at the risk sometimes of losing their good opinion of us), and as a way of sharing with others those things that matter about ourselves, and that give them the opportunity to feel closer to us. As we become more aware and more mindful of our own behaviour (see Chapter 7), we can also become more alert to those occasions when we hide or use the truth simply from selfish motives, or from a desire to hurt or score over others. It seems that the question Christ refrained from answering, 'What is truth?', is one of life's koans (see Chapter 6). Certain it is that, like a koan, we have to keep the question constantly before us. Only in that way will the answer gradually reveal itself to us.

Sexual Misconduct

Religions generally seem to have a very ambivalent and confused attitude towards sexuality. This is not really surprising. On the one hand, the sex act must be ordained and sanctified by the creative power behind all life, as it is the means by which the human race sustains and renews itself. On the other hand, it is closely linked to sensual pleasure, and as such can be a powerful distraction from higher things. Taking its cue originally from religion, society has the same ambivalent approach. Sexuality and sexual symbolism are allowed to dominate the media and the advertising industry, and thus to be placed constantly before the minds of the great majority of men and women. Yet society hedges sexuality around with a range of taboos, censorship and legal prohibitions – so much so, in fact, that it is more difficult to show even a simulation of the sex act in the media and get away with it than it is to show newsreels of actual maimings and killings.

Of course, none of the moral codes laid down by the great religions prohibits sexual relationships for lay men and women. The strictures are not against sexuality *per se*, but against sexual misconduct. However, as with the other elements of moral codes, the definition and meaning of sexual misconduct poses a number of problems. Different religions interpret it differently. In Christianity, for a man or woman to have sexual relationships outside a monogamous marriage is considered adulterous, and thus a very definite example of sexual misconduct. Yet in Islam (where up to four wives are allowed provided the husband can support them) and certain other religions, a man is permitted to have more wives than one. So are men in some branches of Tibetan Buddhism, which also allows women to have more than one husband.

Unless one adheres strictly to the teachings of only one religion, this lack of consensus among the great traditions on what is meant by adultery is disturbing. It is sometimes said that the constant factor across all traditions is that they insist upon a binding contract within marriage, however many partners are involved, and that this usually limits sexual intercourse to those who are a party to this contract. However, this raises questions not only as to what should be in this contract, but whether it should be permanently binding or not. The Roman Catholic Church, for example, thinks that it should. By contrast, Buddhism has no specific marriage ceremony, and in many Buddhist communities (such as those of Tibet and Ladakh), marriages are not seen as particularly binding, and separation and divorce are freely practised.

Civil law is also frequently not in line with religious codes. In Western countries there are no prohibitions against living together outside marriage, and in many instances marriage is seen very much as an optional extra, with dissolution readily available. As a consequence of this muddled and contradictory state of affairs, what are we to understand by the term 'sexual misconduct', and why is such misconduct important anyway?

In all the great traditions, there is a history of celibacy among monks and nuns and among many (though not all) of the saints and holy men and women. There are two reasons for this. The first, as I mentioned earlier, is that sexuality is firmly linked to sensuality, and sensuality is rooted in turn in the physical. Thus sexuality and sexual desire prompt one to identify with the material body, which is contrary to the ubiquitous spiritual teachings that one should free oneself from the body and its appetites, and concern oneself instead with the soul, the Self, the Buddha mind, call it what you will.

At one level this makes good sense. Sexuality is an attractive business, and thus can be a great distraction from the things of the spirit. (I am not concerned for the present with the Hindu tantric path, which teaches that the energy involved during the sex act, when channelled by the most rigorous yogic practices, can itself be a path to spiritual enlightenment.) In fact it is *the* great distraction. Freud rated procreation of the species as perhaps the most important motivating force in life. We do not necessarily have to agree with him to recognize that he had a point. In consequence, for many people engaged in intensive attempts to keep the mind clear, calm and focused upon non-material things, celibacy may not only be personally important, but also an actual prerequisite for acceptance into training.

There are echoes of this in the way that, from the earliest recorded times, one sex has always been dominant over the other within any religion, and able to make the rules that not only govern its own sexual and religious behaviour but the behaviour of the other as well. (Over the last 2,000 years it is typically the male sex that has been dominant, but this was not always so.) This allows the dominant sex to ensure, at least in theory, that the subordinate one is not allowed to become too much of a distraction. Unacceptable as such a practice is to us now, we can at least see the original intention behind it.

The second explanation behind the monastic emphasis upon celibacy is less obvious but perhaps more important. Throughout many of the great traditions the belief has persisted that by abstaining from sexual intercourse, the adept can channel the energies involved into spiritual growth. There are claimed to be both physical and mental techniques for doing this, many of them to be found in the more esoteric tantric and hatha yoga teachings. At one level we can explain this by saying that when one's sexual and romantic energies are turned exclusively towards spiritual matters, they help build up an intense hunger for God, which serves as a powerful stimulus towards spiritual realization. We see this clearly in the writings of some of the Christian mystics, who produced what are in effect intensely beautiful love poems towards the divine, shot through with erotic and sensual images. Even the metaphor of the Church as the 'bride of Christ' carries something of the same echoes.

At another level, we can recognize a belief that sexuality is the manifestation upon earth of the creative power of the divine, and that as such it carries a non-material, spiritual element which can, provided it is not dissipated through physical indulgence, serve as a channel between the aspirant and higher powers. Hence the emphasis in the ancient pagan traditions upon virginity in priestess and priest, and in those ritually sacrificed to the gods. In certain traditions, priests underwent voluntary castration, often at their own hand (see, for example, Frazer's classic work on mythology, republished 1993), an act which was practised even by some of the early fathers of the Christian Church such as Origen. In the Western esoteric traditions, it was considered that magic could often best be worked by virgin youths and maidens in the full flush of their sexual energies.

What relevance, if any, does this have for those of us who are not monks, nuns or saints, but who search for the lotus in the City? It reminds us that sexual behaviour should never be seen as an end in itself, but always placed in context. The most important aspect of this context is the ᵣ   ion of children, and this argues for sexuality within   nd loving relationship that will provide the right   ent for the young children we procreate. Also of   rtance within this context is that sexuality, which is a creative process in itself, should be used to enhance the lives of the sexual partners concerned – ie that sexuality should be an expression of loving and caring, rather than an act engaged in simply for physical and emotional self-indulgence.

It also suggests that periods of voluntary abstinence from sex can be of value to us from time to time, not just on meditation retreats but as part of normal living. Such abstinence is not a form of self-punishment, rather a way of helping us appreciate better the real value of sexuality. Unless we appreciate this value, sex can become like a drug, used as an escape from the boredom of daily life or from anxieties and worries, and thus can actively hinder us from facing and dealing with these challenges. It can become routine, mechanical and commonplace. Like drug addicts, we can find ourselves requiring more and more of it, or more and more variations of it, in order to obtain the same 'high' that once we had.

Abstinence should not, however, be only physical abstinence. Research tells us that on average the minds of young men turn to sex about once every three minutes of waking life. The situation is probably not much different for young women. Anything that grabs the attention as often as this is obviously an obstacle to our attempts to gain more control over the activity of our own minds. The value of such control is spelt out more fully in Chapter 6, but mind control is without doubt a prerequisite not only of spiritual growth but of straightforward mental efficiency. Unless the mind can stay focused upon what it is doing, or upon a given train of thought, then it is like the erratic progress of a rudderless boat. And rudderless boats are unlikely to reach their intended destination.

Alcohol and Other Drugs

There is probably more confusion over this aspect of morality than over anything else. Alcohol, for example, is expressly forbidden in Islam, although it actually forms part of the sacraments in Christianity. Similarly it is forbidden in many Buddhist sects, but I have partaken of it fairly liberally in the company of Nyingma lamas (the oldest of the Tibetan Buddhist orders), and my experience even of certain Zen teachers is that they interpret the ruling somewhat liberally. Although I have not witnessed it at first hand, I have it on good authority that in some Buddhist monasteries alcohol is drunk with great freedom once a year, so that the teachers may observe the level of development of each of the younger monks. I find this idea rather attractive.

The situation is rendered even more confused by the fact that many drugs other than alcohol are used for sacramental and ritual purposes. For example the desert cactus peyote (*hikuri*) is sacred to the Huichol people of South America, who regard it as the plant of eternal life. The Desana people, also of South America, drink an infusion of yagé (*gahpí*) as part of their spiritual practice, while other groups use their own particular hallucinogens and drugs, including coca (from which cocaine is derived). Even caffeine and nicotine are used in certain ceremonies, while the use of hashish has not always been frowned upon in Islam.

So we have a dilemma. Some traditions forbid drugs, others find them spiritually helpful. How can such a dichotomy arise, and what can we learn from it? The first thing to say is that altered states of consciousness can be produced both by deep spiritual experiences and by a variety of different drugs. During a spiritual experience the individual can feel transformed mentally and physically, caught up into a higher state of reality, merged with the absolute, given access to unconditional love and wisdom, and assured of his or her own eternal nature. Sometimes there can even be feelings of being taken up out of the body into heaven, and of experiencing divine wisdom (St Paul mentions just such a case in the Second Epistle to the Corinthians).

Somewhat similar experiences can happen under the influence of certain drugs, in particular the hallucinogenic ones (see for example Lilly 1972, Masters and Houston 1973). After taking even small amounts of hallucinogens such as LSD, visions are sometimes experienced of beings from 'higher planes', along with feelings of universal love and wisdom, of one's own immortality, and of the dissolution of the self into the divine power behind the cosmos. What, therefore, is the difference, if any, between mystical and hallucinogenic states?

This depends very much upon the person who is experiencing these states. It is a mistake to see hallucinogenic drugs as 'causing' the various experiences that sometimes accompany their use. It is more accurate to say that hallucinogens seem to suppress the psychological mechanisms that normally prevent these experiences, just as the psychological mechanisms of waking consciousness normally prevent us from experiencing the dream world. It would be as wrong to assume that hallucinogens 'cause' the experiences associated with them as to say that sleep 'causes' dreaming. Thus even the drugs used by indigenous American peoples during their religious ceremonies do not 'cause' the profound mystical states reported by those concerned (see, for example, Campbell 1989). They arise from some activity of the mind which has been allowed free play by the presence of the hallucinogen in the blood stream, just as dreams arise from some activity of the mind given free play by the withdrawal of consciousness during sleep.

It seems fairly clear therefore that one cannot have a mystical experience just by taking hallucinogenic drugs. Many hardened users of such drugs back in the psychedelic heyday of the 1960s reported never experiencing anything more than shifts in perception (eg seeing the world in rainbow colours), distortions in their sense of time and general feelings of elation. Much depended up[stage of spiritual development when the drugs we

But it may be that hallucinogenic drugs allow certain people to access more readily those levels of consciousness where mystical experiences become possible, just as they will allow one more readily to access those levels where disturbing or even terrifying psychotic experiences become possible. The problem with hallucinogens, quite apart from the fact that they are generally illegal, is that unless their use is embedded in the wisdom and experience of ancient cultures such as those of the indigenous people of the Americas, they are not likely to produce much in the way of either spiritual growth or psychological benefit – rather the reverse in fact. They may, as happened in the 1960s, spread the notion that spiritual experience and psychological health are simply about altering one's state of consciousness in the direction of weird and blissful experiences.

It is worth mentioning though that ergot, a fungus that under certain circumstances can grow upon rye and thus become incorporated into rye bread, is known to have hallucinogenic properties similar to those of its derivative, LSD. Rye bread was a staple diet in many parts of medieval Europe, and little could be done to check the growth of the fungus in wet summers and autumns. Thus, usually without realizing it, many people were probably ingesting small amounts of the drug quite frequently (there are even accounts of large-scale instances of what seem to have been ergot poisoning). If this was the case, it seems likely that some at least of the mystical experiences reported in the medieval world were assisted by the incidence of ergot in the blood stream.

By comparison with the hallucinogens, alcohol, that staple drug of Western society, produces little in the way of hallucinations (except sometimes in the case of chronic overuse!) but plays a useful role as a relaxant and social facilitator. When packaged in wine, it may also have some benefits for physical health. We have had a long love affair with alcohol. In the ancient Greek cult of the god Dionysus

(Roman Bacchus), the god of divine ecstasy, alcohol was used to put worshippers into the frenzied state in which it was thought they could be taken over by the god. And men and women are not alone in this love affair. Animals and insects also have a great fondness for alcohol. Pigs released into an orchard to eat the windfalls show a marked preference for fermented over non-fermented fruit. Wasps spend most of September in a drunken haze. Garden slugs will even drown themselves in saucers of beer left out for just that purpose.

Unfortunately, alcohol also has a very powerful draw-back, and it was against this that spiritual teachers warned. Alcohol relaxes our control over our behaviour, allows emotions to be all too easily aroused, facilitates violence and sexual indiscretions, and renders people stupid, insensitive (and ultimately insensible). Even in small quantities it can encourage idleness and impair judgement. It is therefore hardly an appropriate aid to anyone with serious ambitions to follow the spiritual path. It is noticeable that prohibitions against drug-taking have been more strenuous among communities where alcohol is well known, such as Europe and the Middle East, than among communities where drug-taking involves hallucinogens, as in the shamanic cultures of the Americas, Siberia and parts of Africa and Australasia.

We can conclude from this that the spiritual traditions have always been well aware of the negative effects of alcohol, and probably also of the way in which it can be used as a means of escape from daily life, and from facing the issues associated with normal living and with spiritual growth. One is hardly likely to order one's life more effectively or to become closer to God by lying face-down in the ditch in a drunken stupor. Looking at the host of more modern drugs now in circulation, from prescription tranquillizers to illegal hard drugs like heroin and crack cocaine, the very same concerns apply. Drugs of this kind all too easily become an escape from life, and if, as all the spiritual traditions maintain, life is given to us for the purpose of growth and development, their use can never be anything other than directly unhelpful.

As most of us in the West are unlikely to give up the use of alcohol altogether, the sensible conclusion is not only that we should take it in moderation, but that we should examine our reasons for taking it. If we take it as an escape from our problems, or as a way of giving ourselves false courage or of releasing our emotional inhibitions, then we are doing ourselves an injury. The only legitimate use for it is as a relaxant and as an accompaniment to good social intercourse.

Working in the City

It would thus seem that the five precepts common to most of the great traditions hold up well as guidelines for spiritual life. Provided they are interpreted and applied with humanity, they help us not only to be better human beings, but to avoid many of the distractions to spiritual progress. All of them are as relevant to our conduct in the workplace as they are to all other areas of our lives, and the first three are a clear indication that we should avoid those very common occupations that call upon us, no matter how legally, to kill, steal or lie as part of our duties.

In the context of the workplace there is something else we can add to this guidance. We find it again and again in spiritual texts, particularly those from the East, and it is well summed up in one of the precepts contained in the short spiritual classic derived by Mabel Collins from ancient Hindu writings and known as *Light on the Path*. It is that we should 'kill out ambition, [but] work as those work who have ambition'. In other words, while recognizing the illusory nature of the material world, we should never-theless work hard to make it a better place. If worldly success comes in the process all well and good, but this success should never be the object of our striving, and should be accorded no more importance than any other aspect of the 'controlled folly' of daily life.

The implication is that status, prestige and high office carry no worth in and of themselves, and are no more permanent than anything else the City has to offer. On a personal development level, such ephemera are no part of the search for the lotus of spiritual growth, and are valuable solely to the extent they are used in the service of the spiritual life and the welfare of others.

Other Precepts

Are there other guidelines that can add further help? To answer this, we can look at what in Buddhism is referred to as the Noble Eightfold Path. This advises us to practise:

- *right thinking* – to study and understand correct views on the meaning and purpose of life

- *right action* – which means essentially to observe the five precepts already mentioned

- *right motivation* – to develop feelings of universal compassion, and to wish sincerely to make spiritual progress for the benefit of all beings

- *right livelihood* – it is difficult to follow a socially useful and spiritually progressive life if we are involved in occupations that do little to assist the common good

- *right speech* – which refers not only to the avoidance of hurtful or untruthful speech, but also covers unnecessary speech; the majority of us talk far too much, wasting time and distracting ourselves with idle chatter and gossip

- *right effort* – which refers to the fact that hard work and a degree of self-denial are essential to progress on the spiritual path

- *right meditation* – which is dealt with specifically in Chapter 6, and represents one of the essential inner spiritual practices

- *right mindfulness* – which is covered in Chapter 7, and draws attention to the most important of the links between inner and outer experience

The message of the Noble Eightfold Path can be summarized as *right view, right meditation* and *right action*. If we want to translate these three into psychological language, we can say that they relate respectively to our conscious mind (right view), to contact between the conscious and the unconscious (right meditation), and to our behaviour towards the rest of the world (right action). If we are able to practise right view, right meditation and right action, we will not stray far from the spiritual path.

CHAPTER 13

The Problems of Evil
and Suffering

Views of Evil

OUR DISCUSSION IN the last chapter on the precepts by which the spiritual person attempts to be guided still leaves us with the problem of evil. Bad things happen, often to people (and whole communities and countries) who seem least to deserve them. In Chapter 16 I discuss the so-called law of karma, which suggests that these things are the consequence of one's own negative behaviour, in past lives if not in this life. But even if this law is true, we are still left with the problem of why we behave badly in the first place, and why even the possibility of bad behaviour should exist in the world. The problem is often expressed as 'If God is good, why does he allow bad things to happen?'

One answer that has been put forward at one time or another by most of the great traditions is that there is a positive force of evil which battles against God and the forces of good. Christianity personifies this force in the form of Satan or the devil, while in the East it is given the name of Mara, the tempter. Eastern traditions such as Buddhism and Hinduism also take the view that there are many other forces, neutral in themselves, that can turn very nasty if not appeased by our correct behaviour and observances. In fact in Tibetan Buddhism, the readiness of Westerners to put misfortune down to chance or bad luck is considered a very shallow view indeed. Everything has a direct cause, says the Tibetan Buddhist, and this cause is always linked in some way to our own behaviour.

The ancient Greek and the Norse traditions were somewhat similar, although here it was felt that it was people's tendency to incur the wrath of the gods themselves that led them into trouble. In fact it was humankind's regrettable tendency to disobey – or worse still to challenge the gods and the laws laid down by the gods – that lay at the root of all problems.

Another view, much favoured by some New Age teachers, is that everything in itself is just perfect, and the problem lies in our inability to recognize the fact. At one level, this is clearly nonsense. The reality of suffering is all around us, and those who are bereaved, sick, depressed or affected by a broken relationship are unlikely to find the reassurance that everything is really 'just perfect' much comfort. It is true that at the level of insight experienced by the great mystics of the past such as Teresa of Avila and Mother Julian of Norwich all things are seen to be well, and as working towards our final enlightenment, but at the level at which the vast majority of men and women live their lives, this sounds no more than a pious platitude.

Ultimate and Relative Reality

One way of reconciling the mystic's insight of the ultimate perfection of all things with the day-to-day experience of ordinary mortals is that there are two levels of reality, the invisible ultimate reality which underlies the world of appearances, and the relative reality of this world of appearances itself. Relative reality is illusory if we mistake it for ultimate reality, but while we are immersed in relative reality there is no doubt that some experiences are found to ⸮e pleasant and some unpleasant. We prefer to be fit and ll, to have our loved ones safe, to be happy and fulfilled in our personal and professional lives, and to be physically comfortable and secure. And as we live in the City of this relative world, where the contrast between the wellbeing of some and the sufferings of others is particularly obvious, any discussion of evil must make some kind of sense to us at this level.

Such sense only emerges if we see the problems and difficulties that face us in this world as the means through which our growth and development is achieved. We do not know why the world should be ordered in that way, we just know that it is. In the discussion of the afterlife in Chapter 16, the point is made that to the Buddhist, even heaven is considered as something of a waste of time, because in an environment of perfection, no further growth towards ultimate enlightenment is possible. There is nothing to push against so to speak, and only by pushing against things is spiritual growth and strength attained.

We see this need to 'push against things' if worthwhile growth and strength are to be achieved in every aspect of life. We see it in the development of our physical muscles, in sporting and athletic ability, in the growth of intelligence (which is simply another word for the ability to push against and solve problems), in creative endeavour, and in inventive genius. We see it also in nature. Trees grow tall as they seek the light, majestic mountains are created as one area of the earth's surface meets and pushes against another, beautiful coastlines are created from the pounding of the waves, species evolve and develop as they meet and adapt to environmental challenge, and sleep arises from the fatigue of the day.

Let me repeat again that we do not know why this should be. If indeed ultimate reality can be expressed in an infinite number of ways, then we can imagine that the world might have been ordered differently. But if so, it certainly would not be this world, so such speculation is useless. This is the world in which we live, and one of its inalienable laws seems to be that struggle is important for growth. If this is true in so many areas of existence, it seems natural that it should also be so in spiritual matters.

This does not mean of course that we should adopt a fatalistic attitude, and sit back and do nothing. The need to engage with the world and to try to make it a better place is part of the process of struggle to which we are called. Passive acceptance is of no value to anyone. Certainly, if there is something we would like to change but cannot, we must accept it rather than waste our energies in bitterness and resentment. But acceptance of this kind is not passive. It is highly active in that it seeks to understand and adapt to the experience concerned, to recognize the growth possibilities contained within it, and where appropriate to seek ways of re-employing frustrated energies in other useful areas.

Meeting the Challenges

Living involves making choices, and this raises the whole issue of free will. Since time immemorial men and women have debated whether we have such a thing, or whether we are simply the victims of circumstances and of our own conditioning. Perhaps surprisingly, there is no way of resolving this debate. Even if I decide at this moment to get up from my desk and go and shut my study door in order to demonstrate my free will, it could be argued that this decision is simply the result of my conditioned wish to prove that there *is* such a thing as free will. Everything we do may thus be dictated by our environment and our past life experiences, rather than by any inner autonomy.

The best answer to the dilemma of free will has therefore to be that of the 18th-century German philosopher Immanuel Kant, namely that we behave *as if* we have free will. We must think and act 'as if', and that is all there is to it. In the City, we must believe that much of our behaviour is under our own direct control, and must attempt to extend this control to all those areas where it seems appropriate and feasible to do so. We must not see ourselves as the instruments of a blind fate, or as a collection of conditioned reflexes similar to the tricks performed by animals in a circus.

In other words we must think of ourselves in ways that elevate rather than debase our humanity, and that see us as playing a major part in the shaping of our own psychological and spiritual destinies. Anything less is a major handicap in the search for the lotus, and serves only to build yet more walls to shut out the light not only from ourselves but from those whose lives we touch.

Relationships

Relationships often provide us with our biggest challenges. Much of our life is built around them. Lovers, partners, children, colleagues, friends and acquaintances are the backdrop against which we live our lives, so much so that much of our identity (see Chapter 8) is bound up in and with them. Broken relationships, the feeling of being unloved or rejected by those we care for or those whose opinions we respect, can have a devastating effect not only upon our feelings, but upon our sense of self-worth and our judgement of our abilities.

The problem is particularly acute in the City, where so much of life is bound up in other people – although even in the tranquil world of the monastery or convent monks and nuns tell me that the actions of their brothers and sisters can become intensely irritating at times. And I have myself found that in the course of silent retreats one can experience a sudden fierce annoyance with fellow meditators over apparently trivial matters. In the absence of other diversions and of language to oil the wheels of community living, one becomes acutely sensitive to the mannerisms and the possibly inconsiderate behaviour of the people with whom one is sharing one's silent space. So it is not only the City that challenges us, it is social living itself. Other people provide much of our joy, but at the same time they provide many of our trials and tribulations.

The spiritual teaching on relationships is very clear, although at times very difficult to follow. It is that we become vulnerable when the self enters into our dealings with others. When an important relationship breaks up, it is the sense of personal loss that distresses us. Were we able to think only of the other person, we would recognize that we do not possess them, and that for them the ending of the relationship may be the right way forward. We would even be able to find joy in their new-found happiness. Similarly we would be able to find joy in the growing independence of our children, in the success of our colleagues, and in the lessons learnt from the criticisms of us offered by others. And when people behave badly towards us, we would be able to respond with sadness for them rather than for ourselves.

As I said, this is not easy! It is not a process that we can turn on at will. It can arise only from steady progress in recognizing the artificial nature of the small, limited self, a self that wants always to order the world as it would have it, and that seeks to put itself before others. As our understanding of personal identity deepens and we strip away surface layers in response to the question 'Who am I?' (Chapter 8), and as our corresponding sensitivity towards the needs of others develops, so this process begins gradually to take care of itself. And paradoxically, as it takes care of itself, so we find it less likely that relationships will break up, that children will leave home without a backward glance, that people will seek to wound us through criticism or to take advantage of our kindness. Not only many of our hurt feelings, but many of our actual problems in relationships are caused by the insistent intrusion of that small, troublesome, clamourous self.

Helping Others Who Suffer

In the City, it is often the suffering of others that concerns us most. We see people laid low by bereavement (which is such an important issue that it is dealt with separately in Chapter 16), and by sickness and other misfortunes, and people suffering depression, anxiety and the many other physical and psychological problems to which the human race is heir. We want to help, but are often unsure how. If there are material ways in which we can do so, all well and good, but often there seems to be nothing, and we stand by helpless, embarrassed, angry with ourselves, and some-times resentful towards the other person for putting us in such an impotent position.

In fact there is always something we can do – listen. Listening is even at the heart of the skills of those trained in psychotherapy and in psychological counselling. Listening is a gift we can always give, and of all gifts, it is often one of the most necessary and one of the most appreciated.

Sadly, although the world is full of talkers, it is not that full of listeners. In the City, if we want to help, we must learn to listen. Listening involves several sub-skills, each of them easy enough to acquire, provided we genuinely want to do so. In summary, we can say that listening skills involve:

- a genuine interest in the other person and his or her difficulties

- the patience to hear them out, even if it takes them a long time to articulate properly what it is they are feeling, and what it is that is troubling them

- the self-control not to keep butting in, to have one's own say, to finish sentences for them, to ply them with new questions before they have answered earlier ones

- the ability to demonstrate by body language that one is listening; a nod from time to time, for example, indicates understanding, a smile shows acceptance, eye-contact (though it should not be fixed and intimidating) shows interest and concentration

- the self-discipline to keep one's mind from wandering, and from allowing the eyes to wander off into space

- the ability to convey, from one's general demeanour and expression, sympathy and empathy

- the ability to remember what is being said, so that next time you meet you will not need to go back unnecessarily over old ground

Guidelines for Counsellors

If you can do nothing else than listen well, then you are already a good counsellor. But there are additional invaluable guidelines, none of them difficult to learn. The most important of them are:

- Help the other person to clarify the real cause of his or her suffering. Often they can themselves be rather confused about this. Usually all that are needed are simple questions from time to time, such as 'Could you tell me more about ...?', 'I was interested to hear what you were saying about ...', 'I'm not quite clear what you meant when you said that ...'

- Help him or her to see the difference between cognitive and emotional issues; the former are to do with the way we think about problems, the latter to do with the way in which we feel about them. Often the two issues are closely linked, but to allow emotion to enter too strongly into something that should be treated cognitively, or to be too rational and reasonable about something which is concerned essentially with emotion, inevitably gets in the way of clarification.

- Once the main issues are clarified, try and keep the conversation focused upon them (again often by gentle requests for more information).

- If possible, be empathetic rather than merely sympathetic. Empathy means that you imaginatively experience what it is like to be the other person, sympathy means that you just feel sorry to see them suffering.

- Accept what the other person is telling you without judgement or criticism. If they think you disapprove, they will naturally either refuse to say more, or will try to put things in a way that pleases you; either way, the truth will suffer.

- Be realistic. Your sympathetic feelings may urge you to reassure the other person that everything is all right, or that they must not cry; but from where they are sitting everything is not all right, and the need to release feelings through tears may be a very real one.

- Closely linked to this last point, do not belittle the problem. To you it may seem as if the other person is making a big fuss over nothing, but the other person is not you. To them, the problem is a very real one, and so is the feeling of suffering that goes with it.

- Resist the temptation to jump in with your own ready-made solutions. These may be appropriate for you, but not necessarily for the other person. Even if they are the correct solutions, the other person must be allowed to accept them through recognition of their value rather than be expected to take them solely on trust.

- Where possible, allow the other person to think through to his or her own appropriate solutions. It is the other person who is experiencing the problem from the inside, not you.

- Assure the other person that he or she has your continuing support.

ding these ten guidelines to your skills as a good listener, you will almost invariably be a great help to anyone in trouble. Be sure that if you make specific promises of assistance you keep them, and beware of promising things that are beyond you.

Do not feel that you are a failure if a problem arises that is clearly beyond you. Try and find an agency or a person able to give specialist help, and refer the other person to them (this is particularly important in the case of physical or psychiatric illness, drug abuse, threats of suicide and many kinds of marital and parent–child problems).

One final thing. There are people who, once they have your assurance of help, will proceed to take advantage of you, and consciously or unconsciously begin to take up time which should be given to others or to yourself (for you also need space for relaxation and personal interests). For this reason, it is always best to make clear right at the outset when you are likely to be available to give help, and when you are not. Be as specific as you can (eg indicate that you can be telephoned on Mondays, or each evening between certain hours, or whatever is appropriate). If emergencies arise, these are of course treated differently, but for other kinds of problems, it is fairer both to the other person and to yourself if the boundaries are made clear from the start. The ability to conserve, renew and make best use of your own energies is an essential feature of psychological and spiritual maturity.

CHAPTER 14

The Temple of the Spirit

The Body in Spiritual Life

THROUGHOUT MUCH OF the history of Christendom, great emphasis has been placed on subduing the body and its appetites, so that it is prevented from distracting the mind from spiritual realities. The body has been regarded as a burdensome garment of clay imprisoning the soul in the world of matter, its sexuality has been anathematized, and virginity and celibacy prized as essential for those on the serious spiritual path. All this sits oddly with the biblical teaching that the body is the temple of the spirit. A temple is hardly a hindrance to spiritual progress. For those who live in the City, a temple is in fact an oasis of peace, a place of contemplation and prayer away from the noise and confusion of the streets and the market place. So what part should the body play in the spiritual life? Should it be seen as an aid to this life, or at best simply as the vehicle that carries us through the day, of little importance so long as it functions and does not distract our minds from higher things?

On the whole, the body is not well treated in the City. Look around you (and perhaps look in the mirror!). What we see is people who are overweight, underexercised, full of the wrong food, perpetually tired. We see people slumping as they walk, sprawling as they sit and shambling when they run. We see people abusing themselves with cigarettes and too much alcohol, and driving even the shortest journeys instead of using their legs. We see people who are tense and stressed, frowning instead of smiling, used up instead of flowing with energy, and in many cases old long before their time.

The truth is that we should be grateful for the body each moment of our waking life, grateful that it can get us out of bed in the morning, that it has eyes that see and ears that hear, grateful for the unseen mechanisms that keep us well, heal us when we are sick, and control our autonomic nervous system, grateful for the pleasures of touch and taste and smell, and grateful for the very fact that it is our bodies that carry us through this precious human life.

This tells us straight away that part of any spiritual path, and in particular of any spiritual path followed amid the physical and emotional demands of the City, must be to honour and care for the body. And there is more to it even than this. For our psychology and spirituality both depend in important ways upon the link between body and mind. The Bible is right to teach that the body is the temple of the spirit, and Buddhism right when it tells us that Nirvana, that which lies beyond form, and Samsara, the world of form, are in essence one. There is no sudden break between the spiritual, mental and physical worlds. The ancient Greeks understood the same truth, with their sublimely beautiful sculptures of the gods in human form. Perhaps the supreme symbol of this truth is the resurrection, with Christ taken bodily to heaven (Eastern religions have many similar accounts of such bodily resurrections). The body is not the mis-shapen Caliban of God's creation, but the expression of spirituality in matter. We are indeed made in God's image.

However busy our life in the City, we have a duty therefore both to keep our bodies as fit and healthy as possible, and to understand how they can be used to help our spiritual progress. We are fortunate in that the City now offers us many ways of doing both these things, often simultaneously.

Mind–Body Links

Mind–body links operate at many different levels. For example, the body helps provide the mind with a sense of identity. We live within our bodies, and if we have a bad leg or a bad back, we think of ourselves – in a way *become* – someone with a bad leg or a bad back. Similarly, when we remember the age of our bodies (an unnecessary habit at the best of times), we become a person who is growing old, and impress the fact upon our minds so that we begin to think like an old person.

Furthermore our identity (and thus our personality) is influenced by our body image. Our physical appearance affects our whole approach to life and to living. It affects the way in which we respond to other people, and the way in which they respond to us. It has an important bearing upon our relationships, both casual and intimate. Even a new hairstyle or suit of clothes can make us feel temporarily more confident and self-assured, just as the wrong hairstyle or the wrong suit of clothes can make us feel badly out of place.

Thus the body affects the mind. But the mind also affects the body. When we are worried or depressed, we show it physically, as we do when we are feeling happy and optimistic. Our state of mind may also influence the efficiency of our immune system (good accounts of these and other relevant factors are given in Weiner 1986 and Grossinger 1987), and, as we saw in Chapter 8, an appropriate use of the imagination may actively help in healing us of disease.

At another level, tactile contact between people can have a profound effect upon the mind. The loving touch between parent and child and between lovers, for example, and the expert and caring touch of the

masseur all have highly beneficial emotional consequences. Even stroking a cat or a dog can help to
induce a tranquil state of being, and have a positive
and measurable influence upon physical health.

At a more subtle level, the mind may be able to
control the energy flow within the body, possibly
along the meridians used in acupuncture and shiatsu.
A striking example of this is the Tibetan tumo practice
– the raising of psychic heat. Through the power of the
mind, the tumo practitioner generates intense heat in
the solar plexus, then circulates it around the body to
such effect that he or she is able to sit on ice in sub-
zero temperatures, and dry frozen sheets wrapped
around the naked body.

The eventual purpose of this is to transmute
physical energy into spiritual energy, as is reputed to
happen when the so-called kundalini energy is
aroused by certain yogic practices, and allowed to
travel up through the chakras (energy centres) until it
reaches the crown of the head, where it explodes into
the halo of enlightenment. The practice, in slightly
different forms, is also used by Taoist adepts in the
'circulation of the light' practice (Wilhelm and Jung
1962).

Yoga and the Martial Arts

Philosophers and scientists have for centuries puzzled over
how the mind–body link actually works, but for the
present, it is sufficient to accept the distinction made by
philosophers between *factual knowledge* and *acquaintance
knowledge*. Factual knowledge, as the term implies, means
knowing a fact about something, acquaintance knowledge
means actually experiencing that fact at first hand. I 'know'
there is a country called Argentina, because reliable

witnesses have told me. But until I actually visit Argentina, I have no direct experience of its existence, and therefore no acquaintance knowledge of it. Many scientists and educationalists favour factual knowledge over acquaintance knowledge, and yet we live in and through and by means of the latter rather than the former.

The mind–body link is acquaintance knowledge. We know it from direct experience, because we *are* the mind–body link. In terms of the mind–body link, we are each our own scientist, and what we say about our direct experience of our own minds and of their relationship to our own bodies counts in many ways for more than whether or not there exists a factual theory to account for the interaction between the two.

It was my interest in the mind–body link that drew me to the study of hatha yoga. As I explained in Chapter 3, hatha yoga, though often used as a way towards physical health, was originally a spiritual practice designed to allow the practitioner to gain control over physical energy and transmute it into spiritual energy. Before I had got very far with my hatha yoga practice, however, I happened upon an advertisement for the start of tai chi classes in a local church hall. I was at once interested, because I had just been reading Eugene Herrigel's *Zen in the Art of Archery*, one of the books that has had a deep and lasting influence upon my life. Herrigel, a German professor who taught for six years in Japan, took up the study of archery as a way of entering the enigmatic, contradictory, introspective world of Zen Buddhism. His short book, spare and austere as a Zen painting, is one of the very few by a Westerner to have captured the inner nature of Zen.

Zen archery is a branch of the martial arts (karate, aikido, kendo and the like – Payne 1982 provides an excellent introduction). Although outwardly to do with fighting, these arts are at root spiritual practices originating in Taoism (the indigenous Chinese religion that merged with Buddhism to create Zen) and Zen itself, and designed to develop the inner harmony and awareness essential to spiritual growth. In all of them, the student is learning an art that is not controlled only by bodily exercises, but also by the development and utilization of subtle inner energies which have their origin in the creative force that is life itself.

There are strongly mystical elements to these arts. For example, when describing Zen archery, Herrigel puts it that eventually even 'art becomes "artless", shooting becomes not-shooting...the teacher becomes a pupil again, the Master the beginner, the end a beginning, and the beginning perfection'. Part of the meaning behind statements of this kind is that the archer learns to draw the powerful Japanese bow and to loose off the arrow without a trace of the artificial ego in the action. Herrigel's teacher, Zen master Kenzo Awa, refers to this as 'a profound and far-reaching contest of the archer with himself'. Only if the archer stands ego-less before the target can 'it' – pure energy, spirituality, the creative power of life itself – act through him, untrammelled by the conscious desire to perform, to do well, to hit the target, to surpass others, to meet expectations, which usually underlies all our actions.

The various martial arts are now taught, often to a very high standard, at centres around the City, and when working with body-mind-spirit one would do well to take advantage of that fact. Herrigel's book led me to want to seek out this 'artless art', where action arises directly from the unconscious, and perfection is achieved without the mediation of the conscious mind. In the absence of a teacher of Zen archery, it seemed to me that tai chi, little known in Britain at that time, was the next best thing. (Later I came upon many excellent books devoted specifically to tai chi. The classic is by Cheng Man-ch'ing and Smith 1967, but there are now many others worth reading, for example Lash 1989).

So I took up the study of tai chi. I can still smell the dust of the bare church hall in which our weekly class was held, still feel the sense of suppressed excitement as I turned up for my four-hour lesson, still see my fellow students in their motley assortment of clothes, and hear the soft sound of their shoes on the wooden floor in the silent hall. Tai chi, like Zen archery, involves going through a series of physical postures (known collectively as the *form*) without the intrusion of the ego. One learns the postures one at a time, stringing them together like pearls on a thread, until they form a flowing sequence of strange, compelling beauty. If they are performed with conscious intent, in the service of the ego, they become either showy and flamboyant or awkward and stilted, depending on the practitioner's temperament and personality. If one strives too hard to maintain physical balance, to do things perfectly, 'it', the flow of inner energy, is lost. Instead of the movements performing themselves, the whole process becomes cerebral and of no more value than a curtsey at a garden fête.

I can still see my teacher going through the form, sometimes extending into the space around him, sometimes withdrawing into himself, each posture falling into place like the branches of a tree arranging themselves in the wind. Watching him, I would be aware one moment of the movement, and the next moment of the stillness that enclosed the movement, with no point at which one ended and the other began. There was only movement and stillness, form and emptiness, each dependent upon and arising out of the other, just as an empty vase is both the form of which it is composed and the space that the form is enclosing.

Once, going through the form at one of the weekly lessons, I was more distracted even than usual by ego and mental chatter, and the rueful feeling that 'it', whatever 'it' was, seemed to be ignoring me. In the middle of a particularly difficult turning posture, my teacher saw my difficulty, and came behind me and put his hands on either side of my waist. At once my body was infused with a surge of white light that seemed to lift me effortlessly into and through the difficult movement. Nothing in that movement was done by me. I supplied the body, and 'it' was supplied by my teacher. I had neither read nor heard of the possibility of such a thing. The white light and the feeling of energy flowing through me from an outside source were marked by total unexpectedness. There was no physical force. My teacher's hands rested only gently on my waist, yet the posture was carried out by his mind, and for a moment his mind and my mind were one and the same.

I have digressed into this personal experience to show how we can have acquaintance knowledge of the truth of the teachings that physical energy can become subtle, spiritualized energy. It is this energy, directed outwards, that is used against opponents when the tai chi master is engaged in actual combat. It is this energy that allows the elderly practitioner to propel much younger opponents across the room by laying only the lightest of touches upon their chests, and it is this energy, withdrawn and used to protect the body, that renders him or her impervious to their attempts to strike back.

I have seen Chinese practitioners do seemingly miraculous things with tai chi, but for the City dweller using tai chi as an aid to spiritual growth it is best to think of it, along with the other martial arts and certain mobile asanas in yoga, as a moving meditation which not only assists the health-giving flow of subtle energy but helps one to stay in the aware, mindful, physically relaxed, meditative state when moving around, instead of losing it the moment one rises from the meditation cushion. Even in the early days of one's training, there comes a growth of body-awareness and of self-observation. One begins to watch closely the activity of both mind and body, and to identify physical tensions and the psychological reasons behind them the moment they arise.

In my own case, I quickly identified a small, petulant,

inner child who felt cross if others performed better than he did, or if he thought the teacher was ignoring him. If he was corrected by the teacher (which happened to all of us from time to time), he was back in the infant school, feeling hurt and upset at being shown up in front of the class. If the four hours seemed to stretch interminably, he longed for the school bell and release. If the teacher asked us to divide into pairs for the duo exercises he was afraid he would be the one without a partner. And so it went on, the small child emerging time and time again to take over the grown man, and render tai chi impossible.

Each of these things had to be silently acknowledged, dealt with and laid to rest. And then there came a time when everything disappeared except the postures themselves. There was a sense both of lightness, of floating above the floor, and of being safely grounded within the earth. The elements of air and earth became one, and I flowed through them with the substantial insubstantiality of water. I saw from direct experience how the four elements identified by the ancients come together in the human body, how it is indeed constructed from the solidity of earth, the airiness of breath, the water of blood and sweat, and the fire of inner warmth.

Linking Mind and Body

When physical practices such as the martial arts or yoga are practised patiently over a period of time, the link between mind and body becomes as clear as the link between the elements, or between movement and stillness. No explanation, no theories are needed. This direct knowledge is seen to have far more importance than ideas about direct knowledge. There are things and experiences, and there are theories about things and experiences, and the latter are only clothing placed on the backs of the former. Clothing can be useful in its way, but it always conceals the naked reality, sometimes so much so that we mistake the clothes for the person, and forget that the former are lifeless and the latter life itself.

And as the link between mind and body becomes clear, so the two work in harmony together. The former does not stress and abuse the latter, and the latter does not distract and worry the former. There is an awareness of the body as a dynamic, interconnected organism. No part of the body functions separately from or in opposition to any other part. The body is like a flexible column through which a liquid flows. Allow the column to remain upright and the liquid flows without impediment. Bend the column over, twist it, distort it, pull part of it in one direction and another part in another direction, and the flow of liquid becomes jerky, spasmodic, and is sometimes interrupted altogether. In my work I constantly remind people to be more aware of their bodies, to look at how they sit and how they stand, at how they contort and tense the body, entwine the legs, knot together the fingers. I suggest that they take more pride in their posture, check that the lower back is straight, that the head is held erect above the shoulders, that the knees are relaxed like shock absorbers rather than held rigid so that knee joint and vertebrae feel the shock each time a foot is put to the ground.

Wilhelm Reich, Ida Rolph, Alexander Lowen (eg Lowen 1976) and a number of other authorities have all drawn attention to what is called 'body armour', the way in which the body tenses itself (with the tensions becoming habitual over the years) to reflect tensions within the mind. In certain forms of massage, one can find places of particular tension where the body armour is especially evident, and by working on them produce not only great emotional release, but sometimes unlock memories of the experiences which led to the armour being created in the first place. In childhood we tense ourselves before receiving a blow, or to hold in an emotion such as anger or fear, or to choke back tears, or to bite off the words that parents or teachers must not be allowed to hear. In adult life we tense ourselves for a quarrel, or to resist a rebuke, or to deal with anxiety or frustration. Gradually these tensions destroy the fluid grace with which we are born. Study your posture this very moment. Sweep your awareness around the body. See if you can recognize the truth of what I am saying.

The Alexander Technique (see, for example, Brennan 1991) can also be invaluable for the City dweller who has got into these bad habits, as can the opportunity to work with a good teacher of movement or dance. The state of the body is a very visible indication of the state of the mind. Working on either of them helps the other. I have had the privilege to learn from many wonderful spiritual teachers, and I have never met one who was tense or ungraceful in the body. All of them had a physical presence that reflected harmony, peace and serenity. In their faces there was none of the strain, the lines of tension and anxiety, the worried frowning apparent in so many of the faces that we meet, and that we see sometimes in our face in the bathroom mirror.

The hexagram named Ken in the *I Ching* (that strange book of ancient Chinese wisdom that has an uncanny knack of reflecting back at us our state of mind, and guiding us wisely on what needs to be done about it) tells us that:

> The yielding are without,
> Yet the strong hold the middle.
> Joyous and gentle,
> Thereby truly the country is transformed.

The yielding is the outer form, moving with lightness and grace, and the middle is the mind, clear and focused. In the subtle harmony and unity between them, the country of our spiritual being is indeed truly transformed.

CHAPTER 15

Choosing a Path

AT NO TIME IN HISTORY has a wider choice of paths been open to those who wish to find the lotus in the City. Ease of travel means that spiritual teachers (and seekers) can move between East and West in less time than it once took to go from Bristol to London. Bookshops bulge with books on every conceivable aspect of spiritual and psychological growth. Esoteric practices and techniques which were once given only to initiates after long years of study are now freely available. Every conceivable mix of Eastern and Western wisdom and pseudo-wisdom is to be had (at a price – and usually the higher the price, the less the value of what is on offer). At the same time, Christianity is offered in new and charismatic clothing, alongside the more conventional version. How, in this maze-like confusion, is the seeker to know which route to choose?

One's temperament is a factor. As we saw in Chapter 3, although there is much overlap between the various paths, some of us may be drawn to one which places much emphasis upon devotion (such as church-based Christianity, Islam and certain of the Hindu sects), others to a path of knowledge (such as Zen, the Gelupa school of Tibetan Buddhism and certain of the mystery traditions), and others to a path of meditation and contemplation (such as the Theravadin and Nyingma Buddhist schools).

Dangers in the Path

But before choosing any path, there is an important initial question to ask about them: are there dangers in any of them? The short answer is 'yes'. Such dangers can arise from the teachings themselves, from the people dispensing the teachings, or from both.

No pathway of personal or spiritual growth is without potential pitfalls for the unwary. These pitfalls are inevitable, because growth is inseparable from change, and change involves certain risks. As you grow, you cease to be the person you were. You may not be ready for this change, or it may come too abruptly, or you may run too fast and not look where you are going, or the other people in your life may not be ready for the change (a point to which I shall return in due course). But some paths contain more risks than others.

All true paths lead to the same place (there are many doors into the monastery, as one Tibetan Buddhist teacher put it), but not all paths are true paths. Some were once true, but have now become chocked with the weeds of neglect, so that those who follow them become lost in the wilderness. Others were never true, and peter out altogether or double back on themselves. Some are downright dangerous and lead to the cliff edge, while others, though true, are too steep for all but the best of climbers.

The safest paths are those taught by the great spiritual traditions, tried and tested as they are over the centuries – for example Christianity, Buddhism, Hinduism (in its various forms), Islam (including Sufism) and Judaism. But all these traditions have both an exoteric and an esoteric side. The exoteric side is the open side, freely available and based largely upon outward observance and an obedience to orthodoxy and the decrees handed down by those in authority. The esoteric side is the hidden side, cons teachings and practices taught only to the initi based primarily upon a commitment to personal bility and inner development and experience. In all the great traditions, the exoteric side is the path of the great majority, and the esoteric side that of the small minority.

Traditionally, the esoteric side has been shrouded in secrecy, making it hard for all but the dedicated to find. Much of it is contained in oral teachings, supposedly given by the founders of the great religions only to their closest followers, as they were deemed beyond the understanding of the many. In Buddhism, the Buddha is claimed to have taught the tantras in this way, while in Christianity it is said that Christ taught gnosticism.

Both the exoteric and the esoteric paths have their value, but the esoteric path, by virtue of the profound effect that it can have upon the mind, is both the quicker and potentially the more dangerous. Based largely upon medi-tation and visualization practices, and upon a much deeper understanding of the forces of creation and the purpose of existence, it can present such a challenge to the individual's sense of self and systems of belief that the unprepared mind can become disorientated and even overwhelmed. Esoteric practices, properly pursued, lead to nothing less than a remaking of one's being or, more accurately, a rediscovery of one's true being. In the process, the limited ego to which we all cling can be abruptly swept away (see Chapter 9 for a discussion of the need to 'give God the ego, but make sure it is a good ego').

The danger that the esoteric path, entered into fully, can sometimes disorientate and even overwhelm one is mini-mal if one has a good teacher, but for those working alone, or with an inadequate teacher, it remains very real. Exercises of the kind detailed in this book will not carry the reader too far too fast, although in all meditation and visualization work it is advisable to discontinue practice for a time if one encounters unpleasant visions or disturbing feelings of loss of identity. These are usually merely creations of the mind, but if they persist, it is as well to use meditation *with seed*, that is to meditate upon a particular

The Goal of Esoteric Paths

Throughout this book, and particularly when discussing meditation and mindfulness in Chapters 6 and 7, mention has been made of the small illusory self (or ego). The central discovery on all esoteric paths is that the self we imagine ourselves to be is an artificial construction, the result of conditioning and of concepts acquired through our own experience or taken over ready-made from others. This self is useful enough. Like much else in the relative world, it serves a purpose – in this case to give us a sense of individuality which has strong survival value. But problems arise if we take this to be our real nature, just as problems would arise if the physicist regarded the objects discoverable by the senses to represent ultimate physical reality.

Christ speaks of the need to go beyond the limited self when he tells us: 'He who findeth his life shall lose it: and he that loseth his life for my sake shall find it' (Matthew 10:39). The Christian mystics speak of the same thing when they talk of 'dying to self', as do the Hindus when they teach that we must 'lose the self in order to find the Self', and the Buddhists when they refer to *anatta*, the doctrine of the impermanence of the self. The 'Who am I?' exercise detailed in Chapter 8 helps us to probe beyond this limited self, and ultimately helps us to find (or rediscover) what lies beyond.

What might this 'beyond' be? If we lose our individual identity, then surely we must cease to exist. But such fears stem from the dualistic thinking that believes we can only 'exist' if we stay separate from ultimate reality, the Godhead, Nirvana, call it what we will. Dualistic thinking argues a restricted notion of this ultimate reality, to say the least. And mystics of all traditions tell us not only of the indescribable bliss that comes with the realization of our true nature, but also of the sense of expansion rather than annihilation that accompanies it.

The poet T S Eliot wrote that 'men cannot stand too much reality', and it is true that if we are plunged unprepared into a loss of the small self, we would find it difficult not only to cope with the experience itself, but to adjust subsequently to life in the relative world. However, Hinduism talks of two kinds of experiences in deep meditation, *savvikalpa samadhi*, and *nirvikalpa samadhi*. In the former there remains a sense of the self contemplating the bliss of the absolute, and in the second the self is absorbed into (or becomes – words are inadequate descriptions) the absolute. Both experiences are said to be equally valid; as indeed they must be once we pass beyond dualistic thinking,

We could say that *savvikalpa samadhi* is the goal of the exoteric path, and *nirvikalpa samadhi* the goal of the esoteric. And that these are not two goals but one.

idea such as universal love, or upon a sacred mantra or the words from a favourite hymn or prayer. Alternatively, a carefully graded series of meditative exercises can be undertaken, such as those contained in *A Course in Miracles* (Schucman 1975).

Paths to Avoid

In addition to the great traditions, there are now any number of other paths on offer, some of which present an amalgam of these traditions, others of which borrow freely from them. In addition, witchcraft, paganism in all its various aspects, occult and mystery traditions, ufology, teachings channelled from so-called higher beings, spiritualism, and cults galore all flourish. How does one make a choice from the spiritual supermarkets now open for business in the City? First, by knowing what to avoid. Avoid anything that:

- demands more money than you can reasonably afford; any path that prizes money before people is to be avoided (in particular if you are expected to sign over property or other possessions)

- asks more of your time and commitment than you are prepared initially to give; all paths require self-discipline and effort, but commitments should be in tune with your readiness to enter into them – the same goes for any major changes in lifestyle

- emphasizes your worthlessness, and then promises to 'save' you by obedience to the authority of the leader or of the group (this is a favourite technique for binding vulnerable people into the cult)

- tries to manipulate your thoughts or emotions by intensive psychological or ritualistic techniques without your prior consent, and before you know what you are letting yourself in for and are ready and able to handle them

- insists that you leave your brains behind, accept everything on trust and refrain from questioning or doubting any of the 'teachings'

- belittles or condemns any of the major spiritual traditions

- attempts to probe into your personal life, or expects you to reveal more of yourself than you wish to reveal

- puts pressure of any kind (overt or covert) upon you to abandon your family or friends or your existing relationships; decisions of this nature must be left to you

- in any way appears to lack humanity and humility, in creed or behaviour

Be open but cautious and sensible in your approach to any teachings. The Buddha always counselled his hearers against taking anything upon blind faith. His message was that we should check up on the things we are taught, that we should try them out for ourselves. If they work for us, we should use them; if they do not, we should drop them and search for something else. Christ advised people to 'seek and ye shall find, knock and it shall be opened unto you'. In other words, we should be active and not passive in the spiritual life. Faith should only stretch far enough for us to consider that a path is worthy of our attention, that it may lead to places we want to go, and that we will follow it diligently and sincerely until we have some idea if it will take us to them or not. Faith should not crowd out the spirit of enquiry, or the courage and strength to stand out against things in which others believe, but which are against our own intuition or understanding.

Choosing a Teacher

In many ways, the path and the teacher of the path are inseparable. A good path taught by a bad teacher may be no path at all, while the presence of a good teacher almost guarantees the validity of a particular path (although it does not necessarily guarantee that it is the right path for you). Bad teachers come in many shapes and forms. Some may be patently ineffectual at putting their teachings across or at applying them in their own lives. Others may be sincere but hopelessly deluded about their path and about themselves, while others may be rank charlatans.

One of the first things I learnt as a psychologist working in the field of psychological and spiritual growth is that there are sometimes no limits to our readiness to be misled. We accept misinformation, misinterpretations and misunderstandings which together can leave us with a hotch-potch of beliefs which have no basis in fact (and very little even in credible fiction). We will often believe simply what we want to believe, and it can take great courage to abandon an attractive belief once we have accepted it.

Sincere but misguided teachers can do a great deal of harm. Their sincerity appeals to us and lends a spurious credibility to their teachings. The key question to ask of any teacher is, 'if someone else told me all this, would I believe them?' The answer 'no' does not necessarily disqualify a teacher, but it should give us pause for thought. Charlatans can do even more harm. A charlatan is someone who knows that much of what he or she says is untrue or unsupported by evidence or personal belief, but for reasons of power or money or both deliberately sets out to deceive, exploit and manipulate others. Many charlatans can be highly persuasive. Usually lacking any moral scruples, they deliberately play upon the vulnerabilities, the needs and the loyalties of their followers, and when these followers have outlived their usefulness they drop them with a callous indifference that leaves them even more damaged.

Charlatans can often be recognized because they:

- expect or encourage an emotional response, directed towards themselves personally, from their followers

- deliberately create dependence in their followers

- turn the group against any individual who does not submit to their authority

- are highly egotistical and self-centred (although they may be very effective at hiding this from the unwary)

- encourage an attitude of exclusiveness and superiority within their group towards outsiders

- are far more interested in receiving than in giving

- are more intent upon putting others down than upon building them up
- expect sexual or financial favours from their followers
- discourage personal relationships between their followers and outsiders
- discourage their followers from developing ideas of their own
- insist that their teachings and their various strictures apply to their followers rather than to themselves; they themselves are above and beyond such things
- are capable of acts of temper and spite when crossed
- are critical of other teachers
- claim that they are an exclusive channel for some higher entity or power, and/or that they are 'enlightened' (no genuine teacher would ever make such claims, even though they may be true)

No genuine teacher will ask for unquestioning allegiance from his or her followers, or invite or expect a binding commitment to him or her personally. Zen Buddhism and some other traditions recognize that training stands most chance of being effective if one accepts initially that the master knows what he or she is doing and saying. But like all good teachings, these traditions aim to help people grow in independence and not in dependence, and as the training progresses, so one is encouraged to question and discuss with the teacher, and to feel free to seek another teacher if one is dissatisfied with the answers given.

Is There an Inner Teacher?

As our spiritual practice deepens through meditation and prayer and the attempt to live a spiritually conscious life, we increasingly access a source of intuitive wisdom within the self which further helps the growth of this independence. This wisdom is not the direct result of anything we have learnt or been told, although it can come from unconscious reflection upon it in the way that creative ideas or solutions to problems emerge from the unconscious once we are aware of our need for them. In Jungian terms, we can say that it also comes from the collective unconscious (see Chapter 4), and may become personalized as it enters the conscious mind so that we appear actually to be in contact with another being. (The great Swedish mystic, Emmanuel Swedenborg, claimed that even God the Father himself came regularly and talked to him.)

In the matter of visions and inner voices we have to be cautious, however. Such pheonomena are common in psychotic states, that is states in which the individual loses touch with reality and needs psychiatric treatment. These states are not necessarily derangements of the mind in all cases. Some of them may indeed be genuine mystical experiences which are too powerful for the individual to handle, particularly as we live in a culture which regards all such things as abnormal. Many of the mystics and saints of the past would in fact be referred for psychiatric treatment if they lived today. As part of my work I have made a point of questioning so-called mental patients on what actually happened in their inner world during the acute phases of their condition. Some describe very confusing and disturbing episodes, but others give graphic accounts of profoundly moving experiences, described in some cases as the most momentous of their lives, and on occasion containing information which it seems they could not have come by through normal means.

Clearly, however, experiences of this kind are more helpful if they come to us at a time when we are properly prepared for them, and can integrate them into our normal, everyday life. We have, after all, to go on living and working in the City. If we are not prepared for them, we can be in the position of small children who have strayed into a room where adults are discussing matters beyond their understanding. We also need to be in a frame of mind which allows us to submit the content of any inner revelations to critical judgement. They may not be what they seem. If they insist that we immediately undertake a drastic change in our way of life, or if they ask of us something that goes against our conscience or which appears to be to the disadvantage of other people, we must beware. Anything like meditation, which opens us to the deeper levels of our own minds, can leave us more sensitive to the unwelcome things that may reside there as well as to the positive things. And the former can, at a superficial but nevertheless frightening level, also become personalized. When faced by such experiences, there is no substitute for a good teacher in the outer material world who can help us understand what is happening, and help us deal effectively with it.

Other Paths

A consequence of genuine spiritual progress is that one becomes more, rather than less, tolerant of other paths, and recognizes that none of them has a monopoly of the truth. In fact there are often more differences of opinion within paths than there are between them. Tolerance of other paths is of particular value for those of us living in the City, where so many paths run side by side. In fact, the availability of so many paths is an advantage the City dweller has over many of those living in monastic communities, in that it allows discussions, comparisons and cross-fertilization to take place, usually to the great benefit of open-minded people on all sides. Listening to the interpretations given by people of other faiths often casts light upon one's own, quite apart from revealing the arities that underlie all the major approaches.

Concepts of God can also change as progress takes place. A useful way of illustrating this is to quote a model from Vedanta, a branch of Hinduism made known to the West through the teachings of the Indian sage Vivekananda (Vivekananda 1963, or see Toyne 1983), and by Western writers such as Chrisopher Isherwood and Aldous Huxley (see Isherwood 1975). In Vedanta, which is such a powerful and all-embracing philosophy that Huxley saw it as an expression of what he named the 'perennial wisdom', God is spoken of at three levels. At level one, there is God with form and with attributes, the God we think of as a heavenly father or heavenly mother. At the next level, there is God without form but with attributes, who we think of as manifest in infinite love, wisdom, mercy and creative power. And finally there is God without form and without attributes, about whom nothing can be said, since all descriptions are limiting and confining. This last concept is the Brahman of the Hindus, the Godhead of the Christians, the Nirvana of the Buddhists, the Ain Soph of Jewish mysticism, and it is at this level that many of the pathways complete their convergence. It is often described in para-doxical terms – for example, it undergoes no change yet it is not changeless, it is eternal yet beyond eternity, with-out substance yet not insubstantial, and so on. It both is and is not.

In childhood, we generally think of God at the first level, but once we see difficulties in the notion of a personalized God we move on to the second. When this in turn raises difficulties (eg if God is infinite love, why do we live in a world where bad things happen?) we move to the third. But as Vedanta makes clear, the fact that we are at the third level does not mean that we must necessarily discard the two earlier levels. There are still occasions when it is valuable and appropriate to symbolize God as a heavenly father or mother, or to think of love and mercy as expressions of God. In bhakti yoga (Chapter 3), it is i almost essential. Provided we realize that these lev symbolic (ie that they are themselves yet at the same time stand for something greater than themselves), there is no problem. It is usually only when we *limit* God to these levels, and then find that this leaves us with unanswered questions, that our belief is threatened.

It is sometimes said that each person must find his or her own God. What this means is that each of us must find that concept of God that makes most sense to us, and is of most help to us in living our lives. A Roman Catholic may worship God through the person of the Virgin Mary or one of the saints; a Protestant through the historical Jesus; a Hindu through Brahma (the creator), Vishnu (the preserver) or Siva (the agent of change), each of whom is seen as a manifestation of Brahman, the absolute; a Moslem through Allah, the all-powerful and all-merciful; a Jew through Jehovah, the God of Israel; a Buddhist (in practice if not in theory) in the form of the Buddha, a manifestation of the celestial Buddhas who are themselves an expression of the Infinite. Each of us, by virtue of our culture, our upbringing, our inborn temperament, finds that this or that personification or symbolization of God is the one nearest to our heart. And it is right that we should honour this manifestation until, far ahead on our journey, in this lifetime or in what is to come, we realize that absolute that lies beyond our present limited understanding.

Sharing our Path

I mentioned at the beginning of the chapter that as we progress on the spiritual path we change, and that other people may not be ready for these changes. They may even strongly disapprove of them, and try to put obstacles in their way. This is one of the major problems of trying to lead a spiritual life in the City. In a monastic community, one is with others who are all (nominally at least) travelling in the same direction, but in the City one is with family,

Gods with Form and Attributes

The great majority of the gods worshipped by the various cultures throughout history have been at the level of gods with form and with attributes. There are, for example, the Egyptian gods, the Greek and Roman gods, the gods of the Mayan and other native civilizations of the Americas, the Norse gods, the Chinese gods, the Hindu gods, and the various celestial Buddhas and bodhisattvas who, although not usually referred to as gods, are nevertheless indistinguishable for most practical purposes from them. Men and women have prayed to these gods, received gifts of healing and of other things from them, heard their voices, and seen them in visions. What exactly was going on? How real were these experiences, or should we put them all down to imagination and attribute the gifts of the gods to the power of the mind to work its own miracles?

The gods are, for the most part, not the products of a superstitious imagination, but are real in the sense that they personalize the creative or divine energy that reaches the human mind through the collective unconscious. This energy, as Jung pointed out, cannot be experienced directly by the conscious mind, as the conscious mind dwells in the world of forms and concepts. Therefore, much as the rays of white light striking a prism become visible in the form of brilliant colours, the divine energy becomes transmuted by consciousness into archetypal beings, recognizable and accessible to the conscious mind. In many cases these visions become surrounded in the course of time by legends and stories created by the conscious mind, and become subject to all kinds of confusions and misrepresentations, but this does not negate the original visions of them.

Often the personalized images of these gods are highly symbolic, and we must be careful not to mistake the symbols for naive attempts at realism. For example, Avalokiteshvara, the Buddha of Compassion, is usually depicted with many arms, but these are symbolic of his ability to reach out and help the whole of suffering humanity. Horus, the Egyptian sky god, is represented as falcon-headed, which represents his ability not only to take the believer into higher levels of consciousness, but also to be all-seeing. Ganesha, the Hindu god with the power to remove all obstacles on the spiritual path, is depicted as elephant-headed, as the elephant is the most powerful of all creatures. Dionysus, the Greek god of divine ecstasy, is depicted with vine leaves, to represent his ability to alter the consciousness, while Pan is shown as half man and half goat, to demonstrate the relationship of man to instinctive, natural forces. In all cases, the symbolism of the god or goddess helps devotees to focus their minds upon corresponding aspects of themselves, and thus to bring themselves into closer contact with the divine energy concerned.

friends and colleagues who may be heading off at a very different angle from us, or who may not wish to do any travelling at all.

The dilemma can become so extreme that one may sometimes have to choose between a path or a relationship. At the very least, one may have to face indifference, banter or incomprehension. There is no hard and fast advice that can be given in these circumstances, as each case is different. Sometimes we may be to blame in that we are following a path that excludes those we love, or failing to explain ourselves fully to them, or making errors of choice about our path that others are more aware of than we are ourselves. At other times, other people may be at fault in that they are acting out of misguided emotions such as jealousy, or the defensiveness that comes from recognizing the truth of what we may be saying, and yet being reluctant to put it into practice.

However, although each case must be taken on its merits, there are some general points that can be made.

- If we are following a path in the City rather than in the monastery, then integral to it is an obligation to family and friends; we must not delude ourselves that we are making progress if our spiritual practice is damaging others.

- No one has a monopoly of the truth; spiritual pride is one of the worst pitfalls on any path. We may not be correct in our beliefs; what is right for us may not be right for another. Openness and a readiness to discuss and debate are therefore essential.

- We must neither force our path upon others, nor exclude them from it if they are interested in it; openness (again), and a willingness to share, are vital.

- If we have a young family, it has a priority call upon our time; as I made clear in Chapter 5, the care of young children is in itself a direct expression of spirituality.

- The temptation to bring spiritual matters into every conversation must be resisted. If we have found something special, we naturally want to tell others, but others may not be interested, and we may end up not just boring them but becoming the butt of their jokes.

- Think carefully before deciding that it is your job actively to try and 'convert' others; it is usually more appropriate to make things available to those who ask.

There is no reason at all why people with very different views on spirituality should not live together in harmony and mutual understanding. Intolerance between two people is a microcosm of that intolerance which has led in the past (and still leads) to religious wars and persecutions. The City tests our powers of tolerance, just as it tests us in so many other ways. If we fail the test, then there is something badly wrong either with our path or with the way that we are treading it.

CHAPTER 16

Journey's End

Belief in an Afterlife

THE CITY LARGELY insulates us from death, and from thinking about death – in particular our own death. The materialist-reductionist philosophy that holds sway in the City believes only in a world that can be seen and touched, and as death removes us from this world it has become the most taboo of all subjects, with any belief in an afterlife relegated to the realms of fairy tales and wishful thinking. Yet all the great religions have taught not only the reality of this afterlife but the crucial importance of preparing for it by our thoughts and actions in the present one. Indeed, if religion is to be more than a somewhat vague attempt to regulate the social order, then such teachings must be part of the very reason for its existence.

I am always surprised by the number of people who have the idea that science has largely disproved the idea of an afterlife. It has of course done no such thing. In the first place, it is impossible for science to 'prove' that anything, let alone a soul or eternal life, does not exist. At best, science can only claim that it has found no evidence for it. In the second place, there is in fact a great deal of evidence, both indirect and direct, that strongly suggests that consciousness survives the death of the physical body. The subject is too vast for me to pursue in any detail here, but let us take a very quick look at some of the evidence concerned, much of which, for all its importance, is unknown to the majority of City dwellers.

Indirect Evidence for Survival

The existence of extrasensory abilities such as telepathy, clairvoyance and precognition have now been demonstrated under carefully controlled laboratory conditions beyond any reasonable doubt (see for example Broughton 1992 for a good review of the research). Sceptics who dispute this statement have in almost all cases simply failed to study the relevant findings. These abilities do not fit in with our known scientific laws, and point strongly towards the existence of a non-physical quality in us which appears to be able to operate outside the constraints of time and space. And since death means coming to an end in the time/space world, it seems reasonable to suppose that this non-physical quality is unaffected by it.

Further indirect evidence comes from the fact that, in spite of our detailed and extensive knowledge of the brain and its workings, we have been unable to explain the mystery of the mind, that is the mystery of consciousness and mental experience. The brain operates as an electro-chemical system, but there is no way known at present in which consciousness or thought can be created by electro-chemical means. As pointed out by eminent brain scientists such as Wilder Penfield, we 'cannot assign the mind a position in space' (Penfield 1975), whether that space is inside our brains or anywhere else in the physical dimension. Other experts such as Sir John Eccles (most recently 1994) and Sir Charles Sherrington also report their inability to find the mind within the physical stuff of the brain. In many ways, the mind appears to be a non-physical quality, working through the physical brain, rather than a set of functions created by it.

A useful analogy is with a driver interacting with the engine in order to drive a car. The mind is the driver, the engine the brain, the car the body. Among other things, this analogy effectively counters the argument that brain and mind must be one and the same, as damage to the former affects the latter. Damage to the engine affects the driver's ability to drive the car, but we would be very foolish to assume that this means that engine and driver are one and the same thing.

Direct Evidence for Survival

Direct evidence for survival comes from the communications, received through individuals who act as mediums, which are claimed to originate with those who have died. Anyone wishing to study this evidence in detail can do so in books such as those of Gould (1982), Kastenbaum (1984), and Stone (1993). The weight of evidence is impressive. Certainly there are instances where the information communicated is too vague to mean much, or where it could come from clues picked up (consciously or unconsciously) by the medium from surviving relatives of the deceased. It is even possible that some of this information could be due to telepathy between the living. But there are other cases, in particular those associated with the great mediums of the past such as Gladys Leonard, Leonora Piper and Geraldine Cummins, which cannot be so easily explained away (see for example Cummins 1986). Unless one closes one's mind to the possibility of survival, the most likely explanation of the communications concerned is that they are what they seem, namely communications from men and women who had survived the change called death, and who are still linked through interest and affection with family and friends on earth.

Direct evidence also comes from the experiences of those who have clinically died but been resuscitated. With modern methods of resuscitation, such cases are becoming more and more common. Research by medical doctors and scientists such as Moody (1976, 1978, 1988), Sabom (1982) and Ring (1985) indicates that in some 50 per cent of cases the individuals concerned were aware of leaving the physical body, and (often by travelling through a dark tunnel) of moving towards a bright light. On emerging into the light, they typically found themselves in surroundings of great beauty and peace, where they sometimes met relatives and friends who had died previously. Frequently they were then told that they must return to earth as their time had not yet arrived, or were given the choice of whether to return or not. Reluctantly, they came back into their bodies (sometimes travelling once more through the dark tunnel), and resumed their lives upon earth.

One of the most impressive aspects of these accounts is that the great majority of the people concerned remain unshakeably convinced, often for very many years, that they really died. They no longer feel a fear of death, and seem sure that their lives have been given to them for a definite purpose, often to do with being of service to others. In many cases those involved have had no prior religious convictions or belief in an afterlife, but subsequently many of them feel strongly drawn towards spiritual matters.

Sceptics attempt to explain these experiences away as simply what happens to the brain when it is dying. Not only do such explanations show a disrespect for the people concerned (there are always dangers in telling people that the experiences they have are not what they themselves consider them to be); they also fail to explain how the dying brain can become increasingly coherent as it dies, as witness the emergence from the dark tunnel into detailed and clearly seen 'paradise' conditions. The dying brain theory also fails to explain the similarities of the near-death experience among so many people. Like dreams, one would expect the images (if any) thrown up by the dying brain to be intensely personal and idiosyncratic.

Karma and Reincarnation

As the evidence points strongly towards the possibility (many would say the certainty) of an afterlife, we then come to the question of the relationship between this afterlife and our present one. Is this life a preparation for the life to come as all the great religions teach, and do our present actions influence its nature? Such a question is of great relevance to all who seek to lead a spiritual life in the City. We talked in Chapter 12 about moral behaviour, but it is clearly more difficult to avoid confusions and temptations in the City than it is if we withdraw to a monastery or a hermitage. By living in the City, are we in fact prejudicing our chances of bliss in the afterlife?

The answer to such a question must include some reference to the so-called law of karma (a Sanskrit word meaning literally 'deed'). Originally an Eastern idea, the law of karma teaches that the present moment arises inexorably out of our past behaviours. At its most extreme, and as one often hears it expounded in the West, it insists that we must reincarnate in this world over and over again in order to live through at first hand all the good and bad things we have done to others, and that we must continue to do so until past karma is exhausted and we cease to create any new. Thus our present life in the City, whether it is comfortable or difficult, is the direct result of our actions in past lives.

It is hard to see how this rather simplistic view of karma can possibly be true. It might have made sense in the days when social change took place very slowly, but nowadays, by the time we return in a future lifetime, the very conditions under which we currently cause harm to someone, or refuse to give them help, will probably have ceased even to exist. One answer sometimes put forward is that it is the *impact* of karma upon you that is equivalent to the impact you had upon others, rather than the conditions. But it is hard to see how such a state of affairs could work without a conscious agency overseeing the whole process. Such an agency would have to ensure that the ever-changing circumstances within which we live are organized so as to provide the karmic rewards and punishments earned in previous lives by each of the five billion or so people on earth at any one time – a mind-boggling undertaking, and at odds with the notion that karma is simply an inbuilt natural law.

Another objection is that in order to punish us for bad karma from previous lives, other individuals would have to create bad karma for themselves in this life. You harmed others, and now you must be harmed in turn – but what of the karma of those who do the harming? A third objection is that if the differences between individual men and women are all due to karma from previous lives, how did the process of individual differences start? If everyone comes into their first lifetime with exactly the same innate endowments and opportunities, how did some begin to accumulate good karma and others bad? The explanation that we have all existed 'since beginningless time', or that some souls are 'older' (came earler into incarnation) than others simply removes the whole matter beyond debate. We just do not know what 'beginningless time' can mean, or why (since obviously it cannot be the result of past karma) some souls enter into material existence with a headstart over others.

Whichever way we look at it, it is hard to escape the conclusion that, if we do receive post-mortem rewards and punishments for our behaviour, they cannot be experienced only in the physical world. This brings us to the thorny subject of heaven and hell, but before touching upon it, something must be said on a topic inextricably linked to the notion of karma, namely reincarnation.

Virtually all the great spiritual traditions teach reincarnation in one form or another. It was even an acceptable doctrine (although not universally held) within Christianity until the Council of Constantinople in 553. Even in

modern times, probably more people in the world sub-
scribe to it than do not. It is one of the central tenets of
belief in all the great Eastern religions, and also in the
Western mystery and esoteric traditions (although it is not
taught literally within either Islam or Judaism). I am
frequently asked what evidence there is for such a belief –
in fact questions about reincarnation are put to me more
frequently than any other on the subject of an afterlife.
Briefly, this evidence can be summarized under five
different headings, the first three of which all have to do
with the use of hypnosis.

- *Past life regressions carried out under hypnosis or under the
  Christos technique (Glaskin 1975 and 1978)*
  The evidence produced is impressive (see Christie-
  Murray 1988 and Fisher 1993). However, some of the
  past-life 'memories' thus recalled may be due to unconscious fantasizing, or things read or heard and since
  forgotten in the present lifetime.

- *Reports that psychiatric problems have been successfully
  treated by hypnotic regression to past-life traumas*
  A classic work in the field is by Grant and Kelsey (1969),
  and more recent accounts are given by Fiore (1980) and
  by Williston and Johnstone 1988). However, results may
  be due to the fact that the imaginative creation of a
  fictional past life allows patients to express unacknowl-
  edged fears and repressions, and thus to speed the
  healing process.

- *The large-scale investigations carried out by American clinical
  psychologist Helen Wambach (1980)*
  Using group hypnotic regression Wambach collected
  over 1,000 case histories, and found the details given of
  food, clothing, artefacts, social class etc to be remarkably
  accurate.

- *Small children who spontaneously provide accounts of past
  existences*

Professor Stevenson of the University of Virginia has collected over 2,000 such cases, and in many instances the children give details which check closely with the facts, and which could apparently not have been known to them by normal means. Stevenson's first collection of published cases (1966) is still one of the best available.

• *Sages such as the Buddha who are said to have remembered each of their past lives in detail*
The credence one attaches to such evidence depends upon one's belief in the sages concerned.

Taken together, this evidence seems impressive, but the case is not finally proven. From my own experience, both of regressing people under hypnosis and of being regressed, I can vouch for the authentic feel of the experience, and for the wealth of accurate detail that sometimes emerges. But even if this suggests that some paranormal process is at work, it may not be to do with reincarnation. It is possible that in the course of regression we pick up memories of other people's lives. For example, mediums have told me that they can easily mistake the memories of people ostensibly communicating through them for past lives of their own. Perhaps the best advice is that once given to me by a Tibetan teacher – do not speculate about your past lives; your present one will teach you all you want to know.

What Kind of Afterlife?

Let us return now to the broader question of an afterlife. Even those traditions that teach reincarnation typically accept that there is an interval of varying length between lives. The traditional teaching within Christianity is that this involves a judgement, as a result of which the good go to heaven and the wicked go to hell. Heaven is vaguely thought of as a place where those who are judged worthy praise God eternally, while hell is seen as a region of eternal damnation, replete with a range of hideous physical torments. For the Roman Catholics, there is a halfway house, purgatory, where it is possible to atone for one's sins and to benefit from the prayers of the living, and where small babies who die before baptism find a place. (The ancient Greeks had a similar three-fold vision of the after-life; the good went to the Elysian Fields, the wicked to their punishment in Tartarus, and those in between to the Plains of Asphodel, where they wandered forlorn and aimless.)

There are so many objections to this teaching that many Christians (perhaps the majority) no longer take it literally. The most obvious objection is that such a simplistic view does not square with more exalted concepts of God. If God is by nature complete and perfect, it is unlikely that he or she will 'need' eternal praise from celestial choirs. And if the wicked are doomed to eternal torment, who created the torment or the tormentors? And why should a God of love give life to individuals only to consign them for ever to fire and brimstone?

Other religions also have their judgements and their resulting heavens and hells (and in some cases their purgatories as well). The Buddhists have one of the most daunting selections of hells, ranging from cold hells (apparently much worse than being abandoned naked in the Antarctic) to volcano-like hot hells. The Japanese afterlife encompasses no less than 16 different hells, while in certain Islamic traditions the bodies of sinners are said to be actually enlarged so that their sufferings can be increased. Generally, however, hell is not seen in these various traditions as eternal. In Buddhism, the Bodhisattva Tsitigarbharaja is said to descend into hell in order to teach and rescue all who call for his help, while even those not reached by him are eventually freed for their next rebirth when they have worked off all their negative karma.

Heaven in all major religions is seen as a place where one experiences the perfection (different cultures define perfection in different ways) denied to us upon earth. But in all Eastern traditions that teach reincarnation, heaven is not seen as a permanent state. In Buddhism for example, it is a temporary reward for gaining great merit during one's lifetime. When the merit is exhausted, one returns to mortal existence and starts another round of birth and death. As mentioned earlier, heaven is seen as something of a waste of time, as it is a place without challenge and choice, and therefore a place where progress is impossible. The aim is to progress *beyond* the various realms of form, heaven included, and attain the ineffable state of Nirvana.

Evidence from people who have had near death experiences, together with that received through mediums, also points to a post-mortem judgement of some kind, although they suggest that the immediate afterlife itself may be very similar to earthly life (see, for example, Crookall 1978, Ring 1985, Forman 1989). Some sceptics dismiss the idea of an afterlife precisely because communications through mediums make it sound absurdly like our life upon earth. But just as the present world is co-created by the action of our senses and of our minds upon the energy systems around us, so may be the afterlife. The main difference could be that, as the afterlife is more of a mental world than the present one, it is likely to be even more influenced by thought. So at some levels it may well contain the enchanting landscapes, the houses and golden cities described in these communications, while at others the surroundings may be very much less pleasant.

This suggests that the experience of any heavens or hells may arise from the individual's own state of mind, rather than from any objective array of rewards and punishments administered respectively by angels and demons. The mind experiences the fulfilment of a life of service and selflessness on the one hand, or the remorse and regret of a life of greed and selfishness on the other. As we sow, so indeed do we reap, but the reaping is likely to be mental rather than physical. But whatever form the afterlife takes, it seems clear that its quality will depend very much upon the way in which we live this life.

Life after the City

This excursion into the subject of an afterlife is therefore of great relevance to us as City dwellers. Whatever form we believe the afterlife takes, the evidence suggests that we do survive physical death, and that what happens to us subsequently depends upon our deeds here on earth. Are deeds of the right kind feasible while we continue to live in the City? The message that comes through all the great traditions is that they are, and that in fact the challenges and difficulties of the City may give us even more chance to grow than the tranquillity of the monastery. The message also indicates that these deeds should be of the kind emphasized throughout this book, namely social usefulness and compassionate action in the outer world, and self-exploration and self-understanding in the inner.

But there is something more. Both the Roman Catholic Church and Buddhism teach that our state of mind *at the moment of death* is of great importance. The former emphasizes that we must have made our peace with God, while the latter stresses that if we die in a state of confusion and negative emotion, or with a mind distracted by worldly thoughts or unable to retain consciousness (which may not be outwardly apparent, just as it is not apparent in deep meditation), we are unable to control what happens to us in the afterlife.

Buddhism tells us that we should endeavour to become one with the clear light of ultimate reality, seen just after death, rather than allow ourselves to be distracted by the mind-created, illusory world that presents itself to us, however enticing that world may appear to be. Even divine images of the Buddha or Christ are said to be illusory in the sense that they are ultimate reality personalized by human consciousness (just as we create personalized images of the Buddha and Christ in this lifetime), rather than ultimate reality in its pure essence.

There is a vitally important message for us here. In the City, we typically neither prepare mentally for our own eventual deaths, nor help spiritually those who are dying. What we might call the art of dying has been lost to us. In addition, we are unsure whether or not our prayers can help the departed, whether or not we can (or should try to) communicate with them, how we should mourn for them, and how we should comfort others in their bereavement. Ignorance of this kind about such crucial issues appears unprecedented in human history. Until the work of Elizabeth Kubler-Ross (1975) almost nothing was being done outside spiritualist circles to combat this ignorance. Thanks to her, to the hospice movement and to others, things are now gradually improving, but there is a very long way to go.

Preparing for Death

Before we journey to another country, we usually look at maps of where we are going, learn about the language and the currency, and find out something about the living conditions. It is odd therefore that most of us do nothing to prepare for our eventual journey into the next world. We push the whole thing to the back of our minds even though, as I have tried to show, the evidence that there is a next world is particularly strong.

I have looked briefly at some of the things we know about this world, and given references that are useful for further reading. I have also referred to the compassionate action and self-understanding in this lifetime that are likely to influence what happens to us in the next. Something more needs to be said however about the role played by our state of mind at the time of death. The Buddhist tradition

teaches that the regular practice of meditation a[...]
ness helps us to remain concentrated when de[...]
ches, so that the attention is not dissipated by random,
haphazard thoughts. The same tradition teaches us that we
must not allow worldly thoughts of any kind (particularly
negative ones) to distract us, and that our awareness
should be focused either upon the idea of moving into the
clear light of ultimate reality, or, if we find this difficult,
upon Christ or the Buddha or whichever divine image is
closest to us.

Each day we can also ask in prayer that we may make the
transition through death consciously, with our mind
concentrated upon the clear light or upon the divine image,
and that our passing may take place in a way that helps
those we leave behind. We can ask that no distracting
thoughts disturb us, that we may be in a state of purity and
grace, and that after we have made the crossing we may
become one with (or be with) the clear light or God or
Christ or the Buddha or whatever reality is the focus of our
attention. We can, when counselling others, give them the
same advice. The Tibetans, the Egyptians and many other
cultures had texts which gave the dying careful instructions
on what they must see and do as they entered the next
world (see, for example, Evans-Wentz 1927, and Faulkner
1985). These texts were appropriate to the cultures concerned (it has already been said that the next world appears
to be a world of thought), and we have no appropriate
Western equivalent, but the dying should be helped to
remain calm and undistracted at all times, and to be
assured of their continuation after death. Even if they are
unconscious, these instructions should still be whispered to
them, as there is much evidence that unconscious patients
can be aware of all that goes on around them.

After death, the body should not be immediately
touched. (The Tibetans say not for three days, but that if
this is not possible, the first touch should be a light tap on
the crown of the head so that the spirit exits through what

is known in the East as the aperture of Brahman.) Many traditions teach in addition that the consciousness remains present in the room for a period of time after physical death, and is still aware of what is said and done around the body. There should therefore be dignity and quiet prayers.

Communication with the Dead

This phenomenon is reported in the Bible and in much of the spiritual literature of the world. In the East it is taken for granted that such communication can take place, although in the West it is now only the spiritualists who take this particular view. But should we attempt to communicate, either through a medium or on our own? The teachings from those traditions that accept the reality of communication say we should, but only if it helps the living to resume their normal lives, and if it does not hinder the progress of those who have died.

Provided these cautions are taken into account, success- ful communication can help ease the sorrow of the living, and assure them of the continuity of life. There are many books devoted specifically to communication (for example Beard 1980 and 1983), and there is no space here to go into the subject in any detail. However it is appropriate to say that no one who sincerely wishes to attempt communica- tion should be deterred by the scepticism of others, or by dire warnings that this is communication with the devil. The best advice is to consult a reputable medium who will approach the subject with sincerity and honesty, make no extravagant promises, and have only your interests at heart. You may be given convincing communications and you may not. Nobody knows for sure the conditions that govern such matters. Do not be disheartened if nothing comes. The evidence for an afterlife rests upon firmer ground than whether results are obtained in individual cases.

Coping with Bereavement

In the City, few people turn to a minister of religion or to a bereavement counsellor (and there are very few of those) to help them over the death of a loved one. Family, neighbours and friends do the best they can, but are usually faced with not knowing what to say. Having no knowledge of an afterlife, and no schooling on death and dying within their formal education, what is there for them to say?

The first thing to stress is that grief at the loss of those we love is natural, and if grief is felt, it is better to express it openly than to bottle it up. The frenzied displays of emotion that we see on the newsreels after a tragedy in the Middle East are healthy in that they allow the mourner an uninhibited release of inner pain that is usually followed by calmness and acceptance. They also enable the mourner to feel that there has been a proper leave-taking, another important feature of the mourning process. It is important therefore that the beareaved should know that they can give full expression to their deepest feelings without hindrance or embarrassment. They may also want to talk about these feelings, which may include regret over their own past behaviour towards the loved one, or guilt that they have outlived them or that they do not feel the weight of sorrow they think they should, or are even experiencing actual relief over the death. Conflicting emotions are often present after bereavement, and the reasons for them may need to be brought into the open and talked through.

The second thing is that most people in mourning like to know that your feelings are not just of sympathy for them, but personal sadness over the death. Too much sympathy only reminds the bereaved of the extent of their loss. The sadness of others helps them to know that this loss is shared, even that others require sympathy from *them*.

As to how we should mourn for those we have lost, prayers for their safe passage can be of great importance. It is very likely that these prayers help the departed (if we believe prayers help our loved ones in this life, how much more may this be true after their death). In addition, if the remarkably uniform evidence produced by mediumistic communications across cultures is to be believed, those who have died are very conscious of our thoughts towards them, particularly in the early months after their departure. Our love and our prayers may be an inspiration and a comfort to them wherever they happen to be.

However, if the same mediumistic evidence is to be believed, prolonged periods of excessive mourning may have a negative effect, saddening those who have died and preventing them from making progress into the next stage of their journey. It usually takes around two years to recover from the worst of the physical and psychological shocks caused by bereavement, but we must recognize that our grief is not just for the loved one but for ourselves, for what we have lost. And this aspect of our suffering can be greatly helped if we try to remember him or her with gratitude, and not just with sorrow. Life has a natural rhythm of birth, death and rebirth. Our friends leave us, just as our own childhood and youth and each passing year have left us, and just as one day we will ourselves leave other friends behind. Yet, in its own mystical way, nothing of value is ever lost, and for this we must be profoundly thankful.

The Real Journey's End

I have called this chapter 'Journey's end', but so far we have discussed only the end of the journey of physical life. The end of the journey itself, as far as it can be conceptualized by our limited minds, is enlightenment, the seeing into and entering into the ultimate reality that underlies all other realities. But who knows even whether enlightenment, salvation, the attainment of Nirvana, is really the final goal? There may be undreamt of possibilities that lie beyond. Just as life is eternal, so may the journey be, because life and the journey are perhaps the same thing.

In the meantime, the journey is always just as far as the next step. And the end of one set of steps, the steps of physical life, leads inevitably to more steps, to other worlds, and perhaps one day a return to this one. T S Eliot, a poet charged with mystical vision, put it that 'in my end is my beginning', and that seems to say all that, for the moment, needs to be said.

Conclusion

THE LOTUS WE search for in the City is our own enlightened mind, our real nature, our contact with the ground of our being, our perception of the absolute, our spiritual rebirth, the discovery of our Buddha nature, of the Self, of the Christ spirit. People have given it many names, but the thing (or the 'no-thing') to which they refer would seem to be the same. In the dust and confusion of the City it may be harder to find the lotus than it is in the peace and solemnity of the monastery, but perhaps this very dust and confusion is a necessary part of the search. We may have wonderful insights on retreat or on pilgrimage, in the monastery or in the hermit's cell, but all of these must be tested against the City before we know for sure whether they are real. Far too many golden dreams of enlightenment fade when we subject them to the realities of earning a living, of raising a family, of getting on with neighbours and colleagues and friends. The City is our challenge, our teacher and our quality controller. If the City breaks us, then we can be sure that this is because we still have much work to do.

Even the great sages, when they achieved their enlightenment, came back into the City in order to share this enlightenment with others. Christ trod the roads of the Middle East that led to Calvary and crucifixion. The Buddha walked the dusty paths of India until his physical body could walk no more. Neither great spirit retired to the wilderness to enjoy the divine alone.

In Zen Buddhism, there is a wonderful teaching device known as the Ox Herding Pictures. In this series of pictures, a small boy, symbolizing ourselves, sights and, over many years, hunts the ox (symbolizing our true nature) until he finds him, makes friends with him, and is at last able to ride on his back. But instead of disappearing into the sunset, he returns, by now an old man, to the market place to share what he has with others. In one version, the few lines that follow the final picture go like this.

> His garden gate is closed.
> However hard you look,
> You will not find him there.
> He is down in the market place,
> Teaching wine bibbers and fishmongers
> The ways of the Buddha.

Or the ways of Christ, or Krishna, or of the other divine teachers who have found the lotus, and reached out to place it in our hands.

Bibliography

Arnold, Sir E. (1971) *The Light of Asia*, Routledge & Kegan Paul, London

Ayer, A. J. (1976) *The Central Lessons of Philosophy*, Penguin, Harmondsworth

Beard, P. (1980) *Living On: A Study of Altering Consciousness After Death*, Allen & Unwin, London

Beard, P. (1983) *Survival of Death*, Pilgrim Books, Norwich

Bohm, D. (1983) *Wholeness and the Implicate Order*, Ark, London

Brennan, R. (1991) *The Alexander Technique: Natural Poise for Health*, Element Books, Shaftesbury

Broughton, R. (1992) *Parapsychology: The Controversial Science*, Rider, London

Campbell, J. (1988) *The Hero with a Thousand Faces*, Paladin, London

Campbell, J. (1989) *Historical Atlas of World Mythology*, Harper & Row, New York

Castaneda, C. (1993) *The Art of Dreaming*, Harper Collins, New York

Cheng Man-ch'ing and Smith, R. W. (1967) *T'ai Chi: The 'Supreme Ultimate' Exercise for Health, Sport, and Self-Defence*, Charles Tuttle & Co, Rutland, Vermont

Christie-Murray, D. (1988) *Reincarnation: Ancient Beliefs and Modern Evidence*, Prism Press, Bridport, Dorset

Collins, M. (1885) *Light on the Path*, Theosophical Publishing House, London and Wheaton USA (most recent edition 1972)

Crook, J. and Fontana, D. (eds) (1990) *Space in Mind: East–West Psychology and Contemporary Buddhism*, Element Books, Shaftesbury

Crookall, R. (1978) *What Happens When You Die*, Colin Smythe, London

Cummins, G. (1986) *Swan on a Black Sea: The Cummins-Willett Scripts*, Pelegrin Trust/Pilgrim Books, Norwich

Deikman A. (1973) 'Deautomatization and the mystic experience', in R. E. Ortnstein (ed) *The Nature of Human Consciousness*, Viking, New York

Eccles, Sir J. C. (1994) *How the Self Controls the Brain*, Springer Verlag, Berlin

Edwards, B. (1979) *Drawing on the Right Side of the Brain*, Fontana, London

Eliot, T. S. (1974) *Collected Poems*, Faber and Faber, London and Boston

Enomiya-Lassalle, H. M. (1990) *The Practice of Zen Meditation*, Crucible, Northampton

Epstein, G. (1989) *Healing Visualizations: Creating Health Through Imagery*, Bantam Books, New York

Evans-Wentz, W. Y. (ed) (1927) *The Tibetan Book of the Dead*, Oxford University Press, Oxford

Evans-Wentz, W. Y. (ed) (1967) *Tibetan Yoga and Secret Doctrines*, Oxford University Press, Oxford

Faulkner, R. O. (1985) *The Ancient Egyptian Book of the Dead*, British Museum Publications, London

Fiore, E. (1980) *You Have Been Here Before*, Sphere Books, London

Fisher, J. (1993) *The Case for Reincarnation*, Diamond Books, London

Fitzgerald, E. (1859) *The Rubáiyát of Omar Khayyám*, Fontana Books, London (various editions exist, but the first one is the best; the book is continually in print, and the 1859 and 1868 editions are usually published together)

Fontana, D. (1991) *The Elements of Meditation*, Element Books, Shaftesbury

Fontana, D. (1992) *The Meditator's Handbook: A Comprehensive Guide to Eastern and Western Meditation Techniques*, Element Books, Shaftesbury

Fontana, D. (1993) *The Secret Language of Symbols*, Pavilion Books, London

Fontana, D. (1994a) *Growing Together: Parent-Child Relationships as a Path Towards Wholeness and Happiness*, Element Books, Shaftesbury

Fontana, D. (1994b) *The Secret Language of Dreams*, Pavilion Books, London

Fontana, D. (1995) *The Secret Power of Dreams*, Element Books, Shaftesbury

Forman, J. (1989) *The Golden Shore*, Futura, London

Forman, R. K. C. (1991) *Meister Eckhart: Mystic as Theologian*, Element Books, Shaftesbury

Francis, F. (1985) *The Inward Arc*, Shambhala, Boston

Frazer, J. G. (1993) *The Golden Bough*, Wadsworth Editions, Ware

Gallwey, W. T. (1986) *The Inner Game of Tennis*, Pan Books, London

Garfield, P. (1991) *The Healing Power of Dreams*, Simon & Schuster, New York

Glaskin, G. M. (1975) *Windows of the Mind*, Arrow, London

Glaskin, G. (1978) *Worlds Within*, Arrow, London

Goodman, D. (ed) (1985) *Be As You Are: The Teachings of Bhagavan Sri Ramana Maharishi*, Arkana, London

Gould, A. (1982) *Mediumship and Survival: A Century of Investigations*, Heinemann, London

Govinda, Lama Anagarika (1969) *The Psychological Attitude of Early Buddhist Philosophy*, Rider, London

Grant, P. (1985) *A Dazzling Darkness: An Anthology of Western Mysticism*, Collins, London

Grant, J. and Kelsey, D. (1969) *Many Lifetimes*, Gollancz, London

Green, M. (1989) *The Elements of Natural Magic*, Element Books, Shaftesbury

Grossinger, R. (1987) *Planet Medicine: From Stone Age Shamanism to Post-Industrial Healing*, North Atlantic Books, Berkeley

Guirdham, A. (1970) *The Cathars and Reincarnation*, Neville Spearman, London

Guirdham, A. (1973) *A Foot in Both Worlds*, Neville Spearman, London

Guirdham, A. (1974) *We Are One Another*, Neville Spearman, London

Guirdham, A. (1977) *The Great Heresy*, Neville Spearman, London

Hillman, J. (1990) *The Essential James Hillman* (edited by T Moore), Routledge, London

Isherwood, C. (ed) (1975) *Vedanta for the Western World*, Allen and Unwin, London

Jung, C. (1966) *Two Essays on Analytical Psychology* (2nd ed), Routledge, London

Jung, C. (1968a) *Psychology and Alchemy* (2nd ed), Routledge, London

Jung, C. (1968b) *Analytical Psychology*, Routledge, London

Kastenbaum, R. (1984) *Is There Life After Death?*, Prentice Hall, New York

Krishnamurti, J. (1954) *The First and Last Freedom*, Gollancz, London

Krishnamurti, J. (1976) *Krishnamurti's Notebook*, Gollancz, London

Kubler-Ross, E. (1975) *Death: The Final Stage of Growth*, Prentice Hall, Hemel Hempstead

Lash, J. (1989) *The Tai Chi Journey*, Element Books, Shaftesbury

Lilly, J. C. (1972) *The Centre of the Cyclone*, Paladin, London

Lowen, A. (1976) *Bioenergetics: The Revolutionary Therapy That Uses the Language of the Body to Heal the Problems of the Mind*, Penguin Books, Harmondsworth

Luk, C. (1971) *Practical Buddhism*, Rider, London

Masters, R. E. L. and Houston, J. (1973) *Varieties of Psychedelic Experience* (2nd ed), Turnstone Books, London

Merton, T. (1976) *Thomas Merton on Zen*, Sheldon Press, London

Moody, R. (1976) *Life After Life*, Bantam Books, New York

Moody, R. (1978) *Reflections on Life After Life*, Corgi Books, London

Moody, R. and Perry, P. (1988) *The Light Beyond*, Macmillan, London

Parrinder, G. (1977) *The Wisdom of the Early Buddhists*, Sheldon Press, London

Payne, P. (1982) *Martial Arts: The Spiritual Dimension*, Thames and Hudson, London

Penfield, W. (1975) *The Mystery of the Mind*, Princeton University Press, Princeton

Regardie, I. (1972) *The Tree of Life: A Study in Magic*, Samuel Weiser, York Beach, Maine

Richardson, A. (1985) *Dancers to the Gods: The Magical Records of Charles Seymour and Christine Hartley 1937–1939*, The Aquarian Press, Wellingborough, Northants

Ring, K. (1985) *Heading Toward Omega: In Search of the Meaning of the Near-Death Experience*, William Morrow, New York

Sabom, M. B. (1982) *Recollections of Death*, Corgi Books, London

Schucman, H. (1975) *A Course in Miracles*, The Foundation for Inner Peace, Tiburon, California (This is a work apparently channelled from a higher source, and Schucman never claimed authorship as such. The most recent paperback edition in the UK is published by Arkana.)

Sekida, K. (1977) *Two Zen Classics*, Weatherhill, New York

Simonton, O. C., Matthews-Simonton, S. and Creightonn, J. L. (1980) *Getting Well Again*, Bantam Books, New York

Skinner, B. F. (1972) *Beyond Freedom and Dignity*, Penguin, Harmondsworth

Steiner, R. (1969) *Knowledge of the Higher Worlds: How is it Achieved?* (6th ed, revised by D. S. Osmond and C. Davy), Rudolph Steiner Press, London

Stevens, A. (1982) *Archetype: A Natural History of the Self*, Routledge, London

Stevenson, I. (1966) *Twenty Cases Suggestive of Reincarnation*, American Society for Psychical Research, New York

Stone, R. (1993) *Life After Death*, Blitz Editions, Leicester

Suzuki, D. T. (1979) *Mysticism Christian and Buddhist*, Unwin, London and Boston

Tart, C. (1988) *Waking Up: Overcoming the Obstacles to Human Potential*, Element Books, Shaftesbury

Toyne, M. (1983) *Involved in Mankind: The Life and Message of Vivekananda*, Ramakrishna Vedanta Centre Publications, Bourne End, UK

Vivekananda, (Swami) (1963) *Inspired Talks*, Sri Ramakrishna Publications, Madras

Wambach, H. (1980) *Reliving Past Lives: The Evidence Under Hypnosis*, Arrow Books, London

Weiner, M. A. (1986) *Maximum Immunity*, Gateway Books, Bath

West, M. A. (ed) (1987) *The Psychology of Meditation*, The Clarendon Press, Oxford

Wilber, K. (1983) *Up From Eden: A Transpersonal View of Human Evolution*, Routledge, London

Wilhelm R. and Jung, C. G. (1962) *The Secret of the Golden Flower*, Routledge, London

Willis, R. (ed) (1993) *World Mythology: The Illustrated Guide*, Simon & Schuster, London and New York

Williston, G. and Johnstone, J. (1988) *Discovering Your Past Lives: Spiritual Growth Through a Knowledge of Past Lifetimes*, Aquarian Press, London

Index